6 Rules to Understand the REVELATION

By
C. A. Driggers

Copyright © 2025 C. A. Driggers

All rights reserved.

No part of this publication may be reproduced, distributed, or transmitted in any form or by any means, including photocopying, recording, or other electronic or mechanical methods, without the prior written permission of the publisher, except in the case of brief quotations embodied in reviews and certain other non-commercial uses permitted by copyright law.

Table of Contents

Introduction 1

Revealing The Unseen Realm 8

The Cosmic Battle 33

The Deuteronomy 32 Worldview 59

The Host Of Heaven 72

Applying What We've Learned 88

Has Been Coming Violently 115

Completing The Rule Book 142

The Beast Has A Name: Gog 169

Welcome To The Tribulation 198

1000 years, Literal or Hyperbole? 222

Daniel 7 And Satan's Death 238

Now What 260

Introduction

Why did you buy this book? My guess is that you are interested in the Book of Revelation but find it difficult to understand, and you want some help. In that case, welcome to Six Rules to Understand the REVELATION. Let me begin with what this book is not. It is not a walkthrough of the book of Revelation. We will not be going through the book verse by verse or even chapter by chapter. In fact, there will be large chunks we will not cover at all. Six Rules to Understand the REVELATION isn't a commentary on the book of Revelation. Rather, it is designed to help you walk through the book for yourself. It is designed to give you some rules to follow that will unlock the mysteries of the book. We will look at several passages as we learn the rules and how they unlock the mysteries, but it will be minimal in terms of percentages.

I found the following illustration in a book called Landmark: Exploration of Ignatian Spirituality that I think works here. The author, Margaret Silf, begins her introduction with a story about a salad bowl. She tells of a friend's induction as vicar (a member of the Roman Catholic clergy) in a new parish and of the feast that followed. The members of the congregation tucked into the feast, and soon, hardly anything was left except for a large bowl of rice salad. Eventually, she realized why: someone had forgotten to put a serving spoon in the dish. Silf compares this to the church, which she says is too often like that salad bowl. People are hungry and longing to receive—but where is the spoon?[1]

Maybe it was leftover because it was rice salad, I don't know, but I like the way she uses the full bowl as a way to illustrate the parts of the feast we leave on the table because no one has provided a spoon. This book is about providing a spoon. By the time you finish reading this book, you won't fully understand John's Revelation, but you'll have a lot of important tools that you can use to gain a better understanding of it. You'll have a spoon.

Some of the tools will be universal. They will help you understand the Revelation as well as Romans or Hebrews. They will help you gain a better understanding of the weird things in the Bible; the things churches don't like to talk about. Others won't be so universal.

One universal tool will help us connect the two testaments, which is one of my goals for this book. That thing we call the Old Testament might be old, but old does not mean irrelevant. I think you will be amazed at how often John refers to it in the Revelation.

---

[1] Craig G. Bartholomew and David J. H. Beldman, eds., *Hearing the Old Testament: Listening for God's Address* (Grand Rapids, MI; Cambridge, U.K.: William B. Eerdmans Publishing Company, 2012), xv.

One of the not-so-universal tools will help us see the Revelation as something other than a linear timeline.

Challenging our Presuppositions

This book will give you permission to think about things like monotheism. What is monotheism? Most answer that question by saying, "It is the belief in one God." Does that answer hold up when checked against the Bible? The answer is no. That definition is late to the game and only appears after Christianity, likely because of Christianity.

This book will force you to consider terms like "the sons of God." It will force us to consider things like Genesis 6 and the Nephilim. We will be forced to deal with Psalm 82:1

"God has taken his place in the divine council; in the midst of the gods, he holds judgment."

We will be forced to consider the metanarrative – the overarching account of events – of the Bible. What is the Bible about? Why does God choose a single man, Abraham, from among all men? Why does he choose a single nation and then seemingly put them at odds with the other nations? Why does Jesus need to come? Why does he need to die? What did he accomplish?

Don't worry. We will address some of the key points in the Revelation. We will talk about the beast, its number, and the tribulation. But I'll provide this warning: it may be different than what you are used to.

Let me give you an example. The questions we normally hear asked about the beast in Revelation 13 are:

- Who is the beast?
- Where does he come from?
- The questions I will ask about the beast are:
- What is the beast?
- Have we seen it before?

We will look at the idea of personification. For example, when we think of death and Hades, we generally think in terms of something that happens and a place. Death is something that happens to everyone, and Hades is the place where some people go. But that isn't how John describes them. Death and Hades are proper nouns in the Revelation. Death rides a horse, and Hades follows. They are personified. We will explore that in The Revelation and in other key passages in the Bible.

Now, because I know that some of what I write in this book will be different from things you've read before, I want to tell you what I did to test the material. I began by presenting it in lecture form over six weeks to a group of church leaders whom I serve. People I could trust to push back. They were given permission to be brutally honest and I encouraged them to push back on every aspect they were not familiar or comfortable with, especially those things that disagreed with their previous beliefs and convictions. After the first week we began each session with a Q&A from the previous week's material. Everyone was encouraged to question or rebut what was presented. Once that was done, I presented the new material and followed that with a Q&A. I structured it this way to provide an opportunity for people to ask questions off the cuff, having just heard the material, and again after they had a week to explore and digest it.

After the class, a Pastor in our church asked for anonymous feedback. I wanted to be sure everyone had a free punch. Without me knowing who they were they could ask anything, say anything, and they could call me anything they wanted.

I can't do that in this format, but you should be relieved; those sessions were two hours long or longer. I made no attempts to limit questions nor shield myself from tough ones.

Beyond that, I took this material into another church's Wednesday night Bible study as they went through the book of Revelation. I didn't present the information in its entirety, but I used it in the discussion and tested it among people who don't serve alongside me as those in the original test group did. I understand the level of respect those who serve with me have for me because I am an elder in my church or because I sometimes take the pulpit there. I know that can cloud opinions so it was important for me to test it elsewhere.

The pushback there was spirited but the material stands.

One thing I want you to understand about me is that I want to be correct, not right. What's the difference, you might ask? It is possible to be wrong, but be better in debates or be a persuasive speaker. It's possible to win the debate or the crowd and be wrong about the material or conclusions. I once won a debate in middle school arguing for evolution. I've never believed in evolution. I was right in the sense that I won, but I was wrong concerning the truth.

Here's another way to put it. I'd rather be correct due to correction. If someone can show me I am wrong, I will adjust. I don't need to be right for the sake of winning an argument. I have put this material to the test, and it stands. It's been thoroughly vetted and will continue to be vetted.

To be clear, that doesn't mean everyone who has heard it agrees. Not everyone does. What I am trying to say is that it stands against all current rebuttals and other conclusions about what John is trying to say in the Revelation.

We should understand that some of it is interpretation. Some of the material in the Revelation will not find a consensus on this side of eternity. A quick ride around your community will prove the point. There are Catholic churches, Baptist churches, Pentecostal churches, and others right in your local area, that show that interpretations do not all align, and that's okay on most things. That will be true of this material. We will not need to agree to remain brothers or sisters in Christ. It is okay to disagree about much of this material, but I want you to prayerfully consider all that you read.

Lastly, consider the amount of scripture I use. When you consider this material, line it up against scripture and not against the interpretation of your favorite end-times preacher. Ask yourself if the material stands under the scrutiny of scripture. Use scripture first then consider it against the norms of your favorite system.

One or two notes to close. First, unless noted, I will be citing scripture from the ESV. Second, I will be referring to the book of REVELATION, which is identified as *The revelation of Jesus Christ, which God gave him* (meaning God gave it to Jesus) as simply the Revelation throughout this study.

Are you ready to have some fun?

Revealing The Unseen Realm

This book focuses on giving you a better, but not complete, understanding of The Revelation. That's why we are calling it Six Rules for Unlocking the REVELATION. Like I said in the introduction, I'm not going to walk you through the book verse by verse. Rather, I'm going to give you some rules that will help you understand what John is doing. I'm equipping you to go through it on your own.

Though our focus is on Revelation, the greater goal of this book isn't to give you a better understanding of one book of the Bible. The goal is to show you how deep and interesting the Bible can be and to equip you with tools you can use to dig in for yourself. I want you to become students of the Bible. I want you to go beneath the surface.

The book of Revelation doesn't stand on its own; it is connected to the rest of the Bible. It is part of a narrative. John uses nearly 600 allusions to the Old Testament. That should tell us that the Old Testament might be vitally important to the message John, via the Holy Spirit, is trying to convey. The hundreds of allusions tell us that the Revelation does not stand on its own, it is given on the foundation of scripture. It is part of a larger narrative. To ignore it is to miss the whole thing.

These allusions helped me establish the first rule to understanding what John is seeing in his vision. To take that a step further, I think the Old Testament citations and allusions by the New Testament authors are the context in which we should approach all the books and letters of the New Testament. If we don't understand their Old Testament context, we will not understand the message of the New Testament authors.

What is an allusion?

Most New Testament authors tell us when they are using an Old Testament passage. For example, Paul might say, "As it is written...". However, John just does it without any warning. John alludes to or echoes an Old Testament passage and just keeps rolling with no hint of what he has done. Without a good foundation of the Old Testament, the reader of the Revelation will not know that John has given him a clue to help him understand what he is seeing. That's unfortunate because, as I have already stated, John's use of the Old Testament is key to understanding him. It is one of the rules we must follow.

Here is a list of noting how often John cites the Old Testament:

Torah (The first 5 books) – 82 times

Psalms – 97 times

Isaiah – 122 times

Jeremiah – 48 times

Ezekiel – 83 times

Daniel – 74 times

Minor Prophets (Those short often overlooked books between Ezekiel and the New Testament which include Micah, Malachi, Zechariah, and Zephaniah) – 73 times

I've said all that to set up this disclaimer: You will not completely understand the book of Revelation by the end of this book, but you will be given some level of understanding along with some tools that will help you dig out the rest if you are interested. Even if you aren't interested in dissecting the book of Revelation, you'll learn some cool stuff about the Bible from this book. Stuff that will help you understand it.

Are you ready to get started?

In chapter one, I have the task of elaborating on a topic that most of you believe in but not to the level necessary for understanding the Revelation. In this chapter, I must reveal the unseen realm.

The average church goer who attends church about 16 times a year is comfortable talking about God, angels, and Heaven. That's knee-deep stuff, but if you wade any deeper than that into the waves of the unseen realm, people begin to get uneasy. That's unfortunate because John tells us in Revelation 1:10 that he was in the Spirit on the Lord's Day, and in 4:1, he is shown an open door into heaven and invited in.

That's easy to overlook, but it is vitally important because it gives us John's perspective. John has been invited into Heaven. He has a heavenly perspective. Nothing is hidden from him. Especially not the spiritual world.

If we fail to realize John's perspective, we will fail to understand him. Since understanding him is the reason for this series, will you follow me into the unseen realm? We'll go just waist deep.

Are you good? Can we talk about the unseen stuff and go a little deeper? I hope so.

Since we are comfortable talking about God, let's start there.

God is real, and at times throughout history, He has revealed Himself to man in various ways.

He walked with Adam and Eve in the garden. Genesis. 3:8

He appeared to Moses in the burning bush and to all Israel in varying degrees at Mount Sinai in Exodus 24. To the larger group, He appeared as a storm on the mountain, but to others there was much more.

Exodus 24:9-10 ESV

⁹ Then Moses and Aaron, Nadab, and Abihu, and seventy of the elders of Israel went up, ¹⁰ and they saw the God of Israel. There was under his feet as it were a pavement of sapphire stone, like the very heaven for clearness.

From there, Moses and Joshua are invited closer, but the author either fails, refuses, or is forbidden to give further details about God.

Isaiah sees God in his throne room.

Isaiah 6:1-7 ESV

¹ In the year that King Uzziah died, I saw the Lord sitting upon a throne, high and lifted up; and the train of his robe filled the temple. ² Above him stood the seraphim. Each had six wings: with two, he covered his face, and with two, he covered his feet, and with two, he flew. ³ And one called to another and said:

"Holy, holy, holy is the LORD of hosts;

the whole earth is full of his glory!"

⁴ And the foundations of the thresholds shook at the voice of him who called, and the house was filled with smoke. ⁵ And I said: "Woe is me! For I am lost; for I am

a man of unclean lips, and I dwell in the midst of a people of unclean lips; for my eyes have seen the King, the LORD of hosts!"

⁶ Then one of the seraphim flew to me, having in his hand a burning coal that he had taken with tongs from the altar. ⁷ And he touched my mouth and said: "Behold, this has touched your lips; your guilt is taken away, and your sin atoned for."

Are you still with me? I hope we agree that what Isaiah describes is real and part of the unseen realm.

Ezekiel sees something similar to Isaiah.

Ezekiel 1:4-14 ESV

⁴ As I looked, behold, a stormy wind came out of the north, and a great cloud, with brightness around it, and fire flashing forth continually, and in the midst of the fire, as it were gleaming metal. ⁵ And from the midst of it came the likeness of four living creatures. And this was their appearance: they had a human likeness, ⁶ but each had four faces, and each of them had four wings. ⁷ Their legs were straight, and the soles of their feet were like the soles of a calf's foot. And they sparkled like burnished bronze. ⁸ Under their wings on their four sides they had human hands. And the four had their faces and their wings thus: ⁹ their wings touched one

another. Each one of them went straight forward, without turning as they went. ¹⁰ As for the likeness of their faces, each had a human face. The four had the face of a lion on the right side, the four had the face of an ox on the left side, and the four had the face of an eagle. ¹¹ Such were their faces. And their wings were spread out above. Each creature had two wings, each of which touched the wing of another, while two covered their bodies. ¹² And each went straight forward. Wherever the spirit would go, they went, without turning as they went. ¹³ As for the likeness of the living creatures, their appearance was like burning coals of fire, like the appearance of torches moving to and fro among the living creatures. And the fire was bright, and out of the fire went forth lightning. ¹⁴ And the living creatures darted to and fro, like the appearance of a flash of lightning.

How about now? Still with me?

Let's skip down to verse 26.

Ezekiel 1:26-28

²⁶ And above the expanse over their heads there was the likeness of a throne, in appearance like sapphire; and seated above the likeness of a throne was a likeness with a human appearance. ²⁷ And upward from

what had the appearance of his waist, I saw as it were gleaming metal, like the appearance of fire enclosed all around. And downward from what had the appearance of his waist I saw as it were the appearance of fire, and there was brightness around him. [28] Like the appearance of the bow that is in the cloud on the day of rain, so was the appearance of the brightness all around.

Such was the appearance of the likeness of the glory of the LORD. And when I saw it, I fell on my face, and I heard the voice of one speaking.

What's wild about the scene in Ezekiel 1 is that Ezekiel sees it again in chapter 10. Only then it is a scene from inside the temple in Jerusalem, in the Holy of Holies. Ezekiel is invited to see the spiritual side, the unseen side, of the temple furniture and God's presence in the temple. Sadly, it is right before the glory of God leaves the temple, and Babylon destroys it.

In the case that I've ramped up too quickly, I will back down just a bit with my next reference.

Daniel 7:9-10 ESV

As I looked,

thrones were placed,

and the Ancient of Days took his seat;

his clothing was white as snow,

and the hair of his head like pure wool;

his throne was fiery flames;

its wheels were burning fire.

[10] A stream of fire issued

and came out from before him;

a thousand thousands served him,

and ten thousand times ten thousand stood before him;

the court sat in judgment,

and the books were opened.

Like Moses, Isaiah and Ezekiel, Daniel is invited into the heavenly throne room, but here it is presented as a courtroom. This heavenly courtroom is the exact setting into which John is invited.

Revelation 4:1-8 ESV

[1] After this, I looked, and behold, a door standing open in heaven! And the first voice, which I had heard speaking to me like a trumpet, said, "Come up here, and I will show you what must take place after this." [2] At once I was in the Spirit, and behold, a throne stood in

heaven, with one seated on the throne. ³ And he who sat there had the appearance of jasper and carnelian, and around the throne was a rainbow that had the appearance of an emerald. ⁴ Around the throne were twenty-four thrones, and seated on the thrones were twenty-four elders, clothed in white garments, with golden crowns on their heads. ⁵ From the throne came flashes of lightning, and rumblings and peals of thunder, and before the throne were burning seven torches of fire, which are the seven spirits of God, ⁶ and before the throne, there was as it were a sea of glass, like crystal.

And around the throne, on each side of the throne, are four living creatures, full of eyes in front and behind: ⁷ the first living creature like a lion, the second living creature like an ox, the third living creature with the face of a man, and the fourth living creature like an eagle in flight. ⁸ And the four living creatures, each of them with six wings, are full of eyes all around and within, and day and night they never cease to say,

> "Holy, holy, holy, is the Lord God Almighty,
>
> who was and is, and is to come!"

Hopefully, by now we are comfortable with the idea of God, Heaven, angels of varying names or types, and elders. We've learned that **God is not alone in heaven**.

Do we agree?

As a side note, hopefully, you recognized that John's description of things in Revelation 4 is nearly identical to Ezekiel 1. Things like the four living creatures. They are also like the things we see in Daniel 7. In Daniel 7, we read that "thrones" in the plural are placed, and in Revelation 4, we read that there are 24 thrones with an elder on each.

These 24 elders are sometimes described as representing the 12 tribes of Israel and the 12 apostles representing the church, but I'm no longer convinced. They serve a function that is beyond representative. In Revelation 4, they give praise and worship to God like that of the four creatures (See Revelation 4:9-11), but there are other passages that suggest they do more than that. One of which is found in 1 Kings 22.

There, we read of a prophet named Micaiah. He was a prophet at the time of King Ahab of the northern kingdom of Israel. Ahab was seeking the help of King Jehoshaphat, King of Judah, the Southern kingdom of Israel, to defeat the King of Syria. King Ahab has the favor of all the prophets of Israel except for Micaiah, who tells the kings this:

1 Kings 22:19-23

> "Therefore hear the word of the LORD: I saw the LORD sitting on his throne, and all the host of heaven standing beside him on his right hand and on his left; [20] and the LORD said, 'Who will entice Ahab, that he may go up and fall at Ramoth-gilead?' And one said one thing, and another said another. [21] Then a spirit came forward and stood before the LORD, saying, 'I will entice him.' [22] And the LORD said to him, 'By what means?' And he said, 'I will go out and will be a lying spirit in the mouth of all his prophets.' And he said, 'You are to entice him, and you shall succeed; go out and do so.' [23] Now therefore behold, the LORD has put a lying spirit in the mouth of all these your prophets; the LORD has declared disaster for you."

I would like to suggest that God has a council, called the hosts of heaven, that he interacts with and from whom he gathers information and seeks solutions to issues. Is it because he needs to? I don't think so. He does so because he wants to. How do I come to that conclusion? I'm standing here. God doesn't need me, but God chooses to use me and you too.

Is this idea that God uses people and the host of heaven to solve problems based on one passage alone? No.

Genesis 2:19-20 ESV

[19] Now out of the ground, the LORD God had formed every beast of the field and every bird of the heavens and brought them to the man to see what he would call them. And whatever the man called every living creature, that was its name. [20] The man gave names to all livestock and to the birds of the heavens and to every beast of the field. But for Adam there was not found a helper fit for him.

Does God need Adam to name the animals? No, but he sets it up, and it is presented as if God is interested to see what he will come up with. That makes me smile. That gives me a sense of purpose.

Zechariah 1:8-12 ESV

[8] "I saw in the night, and behold, a man riding on a red horse! He was standing among the myrtle trees in the glen, and behind him were red, sorrel, and white horses. [9] Then I said, 'What are these, my lord?' The angel who talked with me said to me, 'I will show you what they are.' [10] So the man who was standing among the myrtle trees answered, 'These are they whom the LORD has sent to patrol the earth.' [11] And they answered the angel of the LORD who was standing among the myrtle trees, and said, 'We have patrolled the earth, and behold, all the earth remains at rest.' [12] Then the angel of the LORD said, 'O

LORD of hosts, how long will you have no mercy on Jerusalem and the cities of Judah, against which you have been angry these seventy years?'

It is clear in Zechariah that God has sent patrolmen over the earth with the job of reporting what they find. Why? Because he needs them to? I don't think so. **I think this is because creation without a purpose is cruel.** The patrolmen co-labor with God in his work. It is their purpose.

Lord of Host

The patrolmen report to the Angel of the Lord, and the Angel of the Lord reports to the Lord of Hosts. The name "Lord of Hosts" can be found over 100 times in the Old Testament and 17 times in Zechariah Chapter 8. What does it mean?

LORD (all caps) is the name Yahweh in Hebrew. Hosts is a military term. It means to fight, battle, and engage in military battle. Some translators say it this way, "Lord of angel armies." God has armies.

2 Samuel 5:22-25

[22] And the Philistines came up yet again and spread out in the Valley of Rephaim. [23] And when David inquired of the LORD, he said, "You shall not go up; go around to their rear, and come against them opposite the balsam trees. [24] And when you hear the sound of marching in the tops of

the balsam trees, then rouse yourself, for then the LORD has gone out before you to strike down the army of the Philistines." [25] And David did as the LORD commanded him, and struck down the Philistines from Geba to Gezer.

Is it the wind in the trees that David hears, or does he hear God's angel armies going out before him? I'm suggesting he hears the armies of heaven going out before him.

This passage in 2 Samuel gives us a hint of the unseen, but there is more to it than just a hint. There is more to these armies than just the sound of marching.

I want to look at one of my favorite passages. It describes the reality of the unseen realm. It is in 2 Kings 6, but I want to set it up. The king of Syria is trying to run raids on Israel, but his plans keep ending up in the hands of the king of Israel. He is sure that there is a traitor in his ranks. When he looks for the traitor, his men tell him that he need not worry about a traitor; the real problem is that pesky Elisha, God's prophet. They tell the king of Syria, *"He keeps telling the King of Israel the things you say in the privacy of your very own bedroom."* The King of Syria is infuriated and sends *"a great army"* to deal with Elisha.

And that is where we pick up the story where Elisha's servant's eyes are open to the unseen realm.

2 Kings 6:15-17 ESV

¹⁵ When the servant of the man of God rose early in the morning and went out, behold, an army with horses and chariots was all around the city. And the servant said, "Alas, my master! What shall we do?" ¹⁶ He said, "Do not be afraid, for those who are with us are more **than those who are with them**." ¹⁷ Then Elisha prayed and said, "O LORD, please open his eyes that he may see." So the LORD opened the eyes of the young man, and he saw, and behold, the mountain was full of horses and chariots of fire all around Elisha.

Hopefully, I've convinced you by now that there is a Godly unseen realm, but what of the enemy? Is there an unseen realm opposed to God represented in the Old Testament? We are mostly familiar with the enemy in the New Testament, the devil who roams around seeking whom he may devour, but do we see it in the Old Testament, or is it just made up by the New Testament authors?

It isn't made up. The evil unseen realm is present in the Old Testament, and you may have immediately gone, in your mind, to the most obvious place, Genesis 3.

Genesis 3:1 ESV

³ Now the serpent was more crafty than any other beast of the field that the LORD God had made. He said to the

woman, "Did God actually say, 'You shall not eat of any tree in the garden?'"

The serpent is Satan. In Revelation 12:9, John says, *"And the great dragon was thrown down, that ancient serpent, who is called the devil and Satan."*

The word serpent in Hebrew can also mean "shining one." That's interesting because of what we read earlier in Ezekiel 1. Verse 7 says, *"and they sparkled like burnished bronze."* Here's the point. Some want to believe in a talking snake before they believe in a rebellious member of God's heavenly council. The serpent isn't a snake; he is the original rebel. When God curses the serpent, he compares him to the rest of earthly creation because he is cut off from his original post. To word it another way, he is no longer part of God's heavenly entourage. He has been expelled from God's council. He has been cast down to the ground.

The Devil is an obvious one, right? There are others that are far less obvious. Let's look at Daniel 10.

Let me set this up. Daniel has had a vision and the vision has terrified him. It is disturbing. Because of the vision, Daniel does what we should all do when confronted with distress: he begins to pray and fast. He eats no meats, nor delicacies and drinks no wine and not for a set time. Not for 21 days. It is clear that Daniel set out to hear from God, and he would pray and fast until he did. This went on for three weeks.

Hear what I said. It isn't a 21-day fast; it's a fast until...

After three weeks, a man clothed in linen with a gold belt whose face appeared as bright as lightning and eyes that looked like torches of fire appeared to Daniel. Those with Daniel do not see him, but they feel his presence, and they flee to hide.

Then this follows:

Daniel 10:10-14 ESV

[10] And behold, a hand touched me and set me trembling on my hands and knees. [11] And he said to me, "O Daniel, man greatly loved, understand the words that I speak to you, and stand upright, for now, I have been sent to you." And when he had spoken this word to me, I stood up trembling. [12] Then he said to me, "Fear not, Daniel, for from the first day that you set your heart to understand and humbled yourself before your God, your words have been heard, and I have come because of your words. [13] **The prince of the kingdom of Persia withstood me twenty-one days, but Michael, one of the chief princes, came to help me, for I was left there with the kings of Persia**, [14] and came to make

you understand what is to happen to your people in the latter days. For the vision is for days yet to come."

This servant of God (angel, to use a more familiar term) is on his way to Daniel with an answer when he meets the Prince of Persia.

Who, or what, is the Prince of Persia? Man or Spirit?

I'm suggesting he is something other than a man. I'm not sure I've met a man who can delay an angel sent from God for 21 seconds, much less 21 days (Jacob excluded). This prince is a spirit in opposition to God.

What has Daniel done? He has presented us with an opposing member of the unseen realm.

Are you still with me?

Michael, one of the chief princes from heaven, came to help the original messenger, who then successfully delivered God's message to Daniel and departed with the following words:

> Daniel 10:20-21 ESV
>
> But now I will return to fight against the prince of Persia; and when I go out, behold, the prince of Greece will come. [21] But I will tell you what is inscribed in the book of truth: there is none who contends by my side against these except Michael, your prince.

Did you see what happened there? The angel leaves and returns to help Michael dispel the prince of Persia to make room for the Prince of Greece.

For time's sake, I'm going to cheat a bit here and jump into the New Testament. In Acts 17, we read the theology behind what Daniel has described for us. This is Paul speaking:

> Acts 17:24-27 ESV
>
> [24] The God who made the world and everything in it, being Lord of heaven and earth, does not live in temples made by man, [25] nor is he served by human hands, as though he needed anything, since he himself gives to all mankind life and breath and everything. [26] And he made from one man every nation of mankind to live on all the face of the earth, having determined allotted periods and the boundaries of their dwelling place, [27] that they should seek God, and perhaps feel their way toward him and find him.

What we learn from Daniel 10 and Acts 17 is that there is an unseen spiritual side over the nations, but ultimately, God is in control. He created from one man all the nations and determines how big they get and how long they last.

We see it in Ezekiel 38 with Gog and Magog. Recognizable names when it comes to end times discussions.

Ezekiel 38:1-4 ESV

¹ The word of the LORD came to me: ² "Son of man, set your face toward Gog, of the land of Magog, the chief prince of Meshech and Tubal, and prophesy against him ³ and say, Thus says the Lord GOD: Behold, I am against you, O Gog, chief prince of Meshech and Tubal. ⁴ And I will turn you about and put hooks into your jaws, and I will bring you out, and all your army, horses and horsemen, all of them clothed in full armor, a great host, all of them with buckler and shield, wielding swords.

God is speaking here, and he is telling the Chief prince of Meshech and Tubal, his name being Gog, that he will direct him as if a hook is in his mouth. God will lead him to the very spot God wants him to be in.

How so?

Revelation 20:7-9 ESV

⁷ And when the thousand years are ended, Satan will be released from his prison ⁸ and will come out to deceive the nations that are at the four corners of the earth, Gog and Magog, to gather them for battle; their number is like the sand of the sea. ⁹ And they marched up over the broad plain of the earth and surrounded the

camp of the saints and the beloved city, but fire came down from heaven and consumed them...

The hook in Gog's jaw is Satan, who is released by God to do what he does best: deceive. His deception brings the nations to God's doorstep for judgment.

Revelation 20:7-9 is related to a passage we find in Revelation 16.

Revelation 16:12-16 ESV

[12] The sixth angel poured out his bowl on the great river Euphrates, and its water was dried up, to prepare the way for the kings from the east. [13] And I saw, coming out of the mouth of the dragon and out of the mouth of the beast and out of the mouth of the false prophet, three unclean spirits like frogs. [14] For they are demonic spirits, performing signs, who go abroad to the kings of the whole world, to assemble them for battle on the great day of God the Almighty. [15] ("Behold, I am coming like a thief! Blessed is the one who stays awake, keeping his garments on, that he may not go about naked and be seen exposed!") [16] And they assembled them at the place that in Hebrew is called Armageddon.

Hopefully, you are seeing what I am trying to do. I'm connecting the Old Testament to what John is saying in the Revelation. I'm doing it because the things John is seeing are things that have Old Testament precedents. They are connected. Ezekiel and John are talking about the same battle.

I point out the throne and courtroom scenes of Isaiah, Ezekiel, and Daniel because John is seeing a courtroom scene in the Revelation. See chapters 4-6.

I point out God's spiritual army in 2 Kings because we will see the opposing spiritual army in Revelation 9, which is like the one we see in Ezekiel 38.

I'm pointing out the way God deals with his enemies in Daniel 10 and 1 Kings 22 because he deals with his enemies in similar ways in Revelation 16 and 20.

I'm pointing out the unseen realm in the Old Testament because John is receiving the Revelation from the unseen realm. As we said earlier, he has been invited into heaven and, therefore, has a heavenly perspective of the events. He sees the events as they happened or will happen in the unseen realm.

As I begin to wrap up this chapter, I want to be very clear: the unseen realm affects our physical reality. It is not disconnected from our reality.

In Daniel 10, the removal of the Prince of Persia for the Prince of Greece played out exactly that way in the physical world. The Greeks defeated the Persians to become the dominant world power, but God's hand directed it.

When Kings Ahab and Jehoshaphat ignored the prophet Micaiah's warning and followed the deceiving words of King Ahab's prophets, they died in the battle.

The King of Syria never raided Israel again after his men were blinded and treated to a meal rather than a sword. (That's what happened after Elisha's servant was shown the unseen realm)

What John knows, and we must know too, is that the things he sees play out in the unseen realm have physical, real-world consequences. When John sees the four horsemen of Revelation 6:1-8 come out to bring famine, pestilence, wild beasts, and swords, John knows that these events play out in his world and have a very real and significant toll on life.

How does he know? It has historical Old Testament precedence. The same was prophesied by Ezekiel to come against Judah for their sins, and it happened. Ezekiel prophesied in chapter 14 that pestilence, famine, wild beasts, and swords would come against Judah. It did so devastating effects, as we see in chapter 33, and that goes all the way back to God's warning in Leviticus 26 against idolatry. These four judgments are promised to come on God's people for worshiping other gods, the rebellious hosts of heaven.

What has happened to Israel, to Judah, and to the nations individually in the past will happen again at the final judgment of the nations who are gathered against God because of Satan's deception.

Here are the first two rules we will follow throughout the rest of the series:

1. How John uses the Old Testament is critical to understanding the vision.
2. The Unseen Realm is real, and it matters to John, as well as to us if we hope to understand what John is communicating.

The Cosmic Battle

In the first chapter, I gave you two rules for understanding John's apocalypse, aka The Revelation.

1. The Unseen Realm is real, and it matters to John.
   John has been invited into heaven and thus relates to us events from a heavenly (spiritual) perspective.
2. John uses the O.T. and what he uses and how he uses it matters if we hope to understand him.

John and his Jewish audience are very familiar with scripture. They were taught scripture from their youth, memorizing it, singing it, praying it, and reciting portions of it daily. Therefore, they recognize things modern readers do not.

You might also remember from the previous chapter that:

We determined God is not alone in heaven.

- We looked at the heavenly throne and courtroom scenes of Daniel 7 and Revelation 4-5. The plural form of "thrones" is prominent throughout the chapters.
- We looked at the way God dealt with the idolatrous King Ahab and how he desired input from those around him. They are his council.

We learned that God is the Lord of hosts. He has armies.

- We saw, along with Elisha's servant, God's spiritual army in 2 Kings 6 and mentioned briefly the opposing spiritual army of Revelation 9.

We also learned that God sets boundaries and times for the nations.

- We looked at Daniel 10 and learned that before the armies of Greece disposed of the Persian armies, the supernatural prince of Persia was able to resist an angel's attempt to deliver a message to Daniel, However, after 21 days, the prince of Persia's resistance was thwarted by Michael, an archangel, and the message was delivered.
- We also looked at Acts 17 where God's sovereignty over the nations is explicitly stated. With that recap laid out, let's look at Acts 17:26.

Acts 17:26 ESV

26 And he made from one man every nation of mankind to live on all the face of the earth, having determined allotted periods and the boundaries of their dwelling place....

From one man, meaning Adam, God brings about every nation and determines their length of time and their allotted space. The Old Testament gives us a brief record of this. Paul is referring to Genesis 11, where God split the people, separating them by language and spreading them out. This was done because, on their own, they did not obey the command to spread out and be fruitful. Instead, they chose a place and began to build a city, and a tower, (or a temple as some scholars suggest). This is the Babel incident.

In Deuteronomy 32:8, we read how God judges them.

> Deuteronomy 32:8 ESV
>
> [8] When the Most High gave to the nations their inheritance, when he divided mankind, he fixed the borders of the peoples according to the number of the sons of God.

If you have the NKJV or other similar versions, your translation might read "sons of Israel." Because of space constraints, I won't elaborate in this chapter, but there is good evidence that tells us the correct translation is "sons of God." (I will discuss it elsewhere. It is a vital piece.)

When God separated the people in Genesis 11, he chose to rule over them by way of government. He would be king, and his sons would be coregents ruling over other kingdoms at the same time.

Deuteronomy 32:9 tells us he kept Israel for himself.

Deuteronomy 32:9 ESV

⁹ But the LORD's portion is his people, Jacob his allotted heritage.

Jacob, Abraham's grandson, represents Israel. In fact, Jacob's name was changed to Israel. Israel didn't become a nation until long after the events of Genesis 11. In fact, it is Genesis 12 where God chooses Abraham to be the father of the nation of Israel.

I'm pointing this out because I want us to understand what Revelation is about. I want us to see that there is more at stake than saving souls when Christ is on the cross. While that is important, it isn't the only thing happening. There are other problems that Christ came to fix, including the issue that God's sons, the sons that he put over the nations, did not do as they were commanded.

Consider Psalm 82. It is only eight verses, so I am going to include the whole thing. But I will pause after verse 1 for a brief explanation.

Psalm 82 ESV

¹ God has taken his place in the divine council; in the midst of the gods, he holds judgment:

The very first word we see in this verse is the Hebrew word Elohim, a term used of God, Yahweh God, the most-high God, the God of Israel, but elohim is also the word used for gods in the second line, "in the midst of the elohim he holds judgment," "in the midst of the gods, he (God) holds judgment."

Has the psalmist (Asaph) lost his mind? Does he know what he is talking about? He hasn't lost his mind, and yes, he knows what he is talking about. Let me explain.

Elohim is a term used in the Old Testament for beings that are not of earth. God is called elohim, and so are others in the Old Testament. But God is also called Yahweh, while no other being is called Yahweh. God is alone in that distinction. God, Yahweh, is the creator, while all other elohim are his creation.

The word elohim in the Old Testament is like the New Testament language many of us are very familiar with: angels, demons, powers, principalities, thrones, and dominions (Ephesians 6:12). All these things represent the members of the unseen realm in their varying forms and offices. They are elohim.

Let me be very clear. There is only one elohim worthy of worship. That is Yahweh, the God of Israel, but there are many elohim that serve him and his purpose. Still with me?

Psalm 82

¹ God has taken his place in the divine council; in the midst of the gods, he holds judgment:

² "How long will you judge unjustly and show partiality to the wicked? *Selah*

³ Give justice to the weak and the fatherless; maintain the rights of the afflicted and the destitute.

⁴ Rescue the weak and the needy; deliver them from the hand of the wicked."

⁵ They have neither knowledge nor understanding, ; they walk about in darkness; all the foundations of the earth are shaken.

⁶ I said, "You are gods, sons of the Most High, all of you;

⁷ nevertheless, like men, you shall die, and fall like any prince."

⁸ Arise, O God, judge the earth; for you shall inherit all the nations!

Later, take the time to read Psalm 82 and listen to the different voices in the chapter. You'll find that the psalmist, the narrator so to speak, opens and closes the passages in Verses 1 and 8, while Verses 2 through 7 are God speaking. It's a worthwhile practice to slow down enough to catch who is speaking when we are reading the Psalms.

Here is what we learn from Psalm 82. The members of the unseen realm have free will. The sons of God, the elohim, that God put over the nations in Deuteronomy 32, didn't do as they were directed. They rebelled, and God is judging them. This judgment on the rebellious sons of God, is the backdrop of Revelation, and it is vitally important to understanding what John is writing.

Let me show you.

In Isaiah 24:21, we read:

> Isaiah 24:21
>
> On that day the LORD will punish the host of heaven, in heaven, and the kings of the earth, on the earth.

The host of heaven are who I am talking about. God will judge the host of heaven in heaven.

In the previous chapter, we discussed the meaning of *host*. It's a military term meaning to go to battle. We also looked at the *"Lord of Host"* or *"Lord of angel armies."* The Lord of angel armies will march against the rebellious host (armies) of heaven.

It is an idea clearly stated by John in Revelation 12.

> Revelation 12:7-9 ESV
>
> [7] Now war arose in heaven, Michael and his angels fighting against the dragon. And the dragon and his

angels fought back, [8] but he was defeated, and there was no longer any place for them in heaven. [9] And the great dragon was thrown down, that ancient serpent, who is called the devil and Satan, the deceiver of the whole world—he was thrown down to the earth, and his angels were thrown down with him.

Prior to that, in verse 4, we read:

Revelation 12:4

[4] His tail swept down a third of the stars of heaven and cast them to the earth....

I have a question for you about the stars. Did the dragon, who is Satan, cast down a third of the literal stars, or are the stars his armies, as is suggested in Verses 7-9? They were his armies, defeated by Michael and cast out of heaven. John explains what he says in Verse 4 about the stars with Verses 7-9. The stars in Verse 4 are Satan's angels.

When we read verses like this:

Isaiah 34:4 ESV

All the host of heaven shall rot away, and the skies roll up like a scroll. All their host shall fall, as leaves fall from the vine, like leaves falling from the fig tree.

And:

Isaiah 13:10 ESV

¹⁰ For the stars of the heavens and their constellations will not give their light; the sun will be dark at its rising, and the moon will not shed its light.

We need to pause and ask ourselves what is in the mind of the author. Does he mean to say that stars will fall from heaven and the sky will go black as a result, or is he conveying to us that God is judging the rebellious host of heaven, the fallen sons of God?

Is John being literal in a physical world sense when he writes:

Revelation 6:12-14 ESV

¹² When he opened the sixth seal, I looked, and behold, there was a great earthquake, and the sun became black as sackcloth, the full moon became like blood, ¹³ and the stars of the sky fell to the earth as the fig tree sheds its winter fruit when shaken by a gale. ¹⁴ The sky vanished like a scroll that is being rolled up, and every mountain and island was removed from its place.

You might recognize the language John borrows from Isaiah 34:4 *"and the skies roll up like a scroll."*

Is John being literal when he says:

Revelation 8:8 ESV

...and something like a great mountain, burning with fire, was thrown into the sea, and a third of the sea became blood.

Is he describing the physical world or the unseen realm when he records:

Revelation 8:10 ESV

...and a great star fell from heaven, blazing like a torch, and it fell on a third of the rivers and on the springs of water.

What about this:

Revelation 8:12 ESV

...and a third of the sun was struck, and a third of the moon, and a third of the stars, so that a third of their light might be darkened, and a third of the day might be kept from shining, and likewise a third of the night.

Is he describing the physical world or the unseen realm?

I suggest that he is describing the unseen realm just as Isaiah was when he was prophesying the fall of Babylon to the Medes in Isaiah 13. In Isaiah 13:10, as referenced earlier, we are told the stars stop shining, and in verse 13, we are told the world was shaken out of its place. Did that happen in the physical world when Babylon fell to the Medes? No. How do we know? Well, we know because the world still exists. We're still here. But did it happen among the host of heaven? Yes, the prince of Babylon was removed from his position by the prince of the Medes by the hand of God. The same type of thing is described in Daniel 10, where the Prince of Persia is removed to make way for the Prince of Greece.

The stars and the host of heaven often represent the unseen realm. Consider this:

> Revelation 9:1
>
> I saw a star fallen from heaven to earth, and he was given the key to the shaft of the bottomless pit.

How does that play out in our world? It doesn't. It happens in the unseen realm. John is describing from a heavenly perspective something that will have real-world consequences, but not exactly as he records it. It's not a star or a comet; it is a spiritual member of the unseen realm. It is an elohim. You see, you don't give keys to a comet or a star.

Earlier, I said there was more at stake on the cross than saving souls. That's why I bring all this up. The cross and resurrection were a battle of epic proportions that is playing out in the unseen realm in ways that we never concentrate on. The battle begins at Jesus' birth, Revelation 12, but it kicks into high gear at the cross. You see, Jesus isn't sleeping for three days in the tomb. Rather, Jesus kicks in the Gates of Hell and tells the fallen Elohim, "I'm here to take this whole thing back for my father." In the Revelation, John gives us a bird's eye view of how it is playing out.

Jesus came to reestablish the kingdom of God, and it began with John the Baptist.

Consider the following from Matthew 11.

Before you do, let me offer a brief apology and explanation, I know you want to learn about the Revelation, and thus far I've only briefly explained a few passages. Here's why: The Revelation is not a stand-alone story. It is the last chapter of a story that starts in Genesis 1. Skipping to the end with hopes of understanding just that book is a mistake. The story must be set up to understand the meaning of The Revelation. You need the context. You need to know the characters. You need to know the plot. You need to know it is the final battle in a war as old as human history.

Jesus isn't **just** saving souls; he is restoring Eden. He isn't just resurrecting souls; he is resurrecting his plan for creation itself. Still with me?

> Matthew 11:12 ESV
>
> From the days of John the Baptist, until now, the kingdom of heaven has suffered violence, and the violent take it by force.

Your Bible may have a footnote on this verse right after the word violence. It's there because scholars realize that there is some ambiguity in the translation. There are options. If you have the NIV, for example, your Bible will say something very different.

The footnote in the ESV says, "or, has been coming violently." That gives us permission to look at the verse again.

"From the days of John the Baptist until now, the kingdom of heaven has been coming violently, and the violent take it by force."

Oh wow. That puts a different spin on it. When we read it like that, we see some resemblance to the things John presents in the Revelation. Jesus isn't just the lamb to be slaughtered; he's the Lion of the tribe of Judah and the strong arm of the Lord coming to reclaim what belongs to his Father.

Let's look.

Isaiah 51:9-10

[9] Awake, awake, put on strength,

O arm of the LORD;

awake, as in days of old,

the generations of long ago.

Was it not you who cut Rahab in pieces,

> who pierced the dragon?
>
> ¹⁰ Was it not you who dried up the sea,
>
> the waters of the great deep,
>
> who made the depths of the sea a way
>
> for the redeemed to pass over?

Do you remember who the dragon is? We identified The dragon last week from Revelation 12:9. It is Satan. The dragon represents God's enemies, and Christ is the representation of God's strength on earth. Christ is God's arm of strength. He came to fulfill God's will and the enemy, the dragon, could not stop him.

When Mary, the mother of Jesus, and her aunt Elizabeth met, their babies still in their wombs, Elizabeth testifies that John leaped in her womb in the presence of their Lord, and Luke records for us that Mary burst forth with praise to God, saying, "He [God] has shown strength with his arm..."

You see, we have done a great job of picturing Jesus as the lamb going to the slaughter, but he is the Lord's strong arm. He is a warrior. He is a victor. There is a lion in the lamb, and if we listen, we will hear the roar of the lion.

Care to hear him roar? Good, because I want you to hear him. You see, Jesus is on a secret mission, and occasionally, it comes to the surface.

In Mark Chapter 1, Jesus is calling his first disciples when he comes across a demon-possessed man.

Mark 1:24-25 ESV

²⁴ "What have you to do with us, Jesus of Nazareth? Have you come to destroy us? I know who you are—the Holy One of God." ²⁵ But Jesus rebuked him, saying, "Be silent, and come out of him!"

Come on! Do you see what happens there? Demons recognize who Jesus is, the Holy One of God, but Jesus muzzles the demons and then casts them out.

Did you hear the growl? It might be low, but it's there.

It gets a little louder in Luke 8 when the Lion is approached by a man full of demons among the tombs.

Luke 8:28-33 ESV

²⁸ When he saw Jesus, he cried out and fell down before him and said with a loud voice, "What have you to do with me, Jesus, Son of the Most High God? **I beg you, do not torment me.**" ²⁹ For he had commanded the unclean spirit to come out of the man. (For many a time, it had seized him. He was kept under guard and bound with chains and shackles, but he would break the bonds and be driven by the demon into the desert.) ³⁰ Jesus then asked him, "What is your name?" And he

said, "Legion," for many demons had entered him. [31] **And they begged him not to command them to depart into the abyss.** [32] Now, a large herd of pigs was feeding there on the hillside, and they begged him to let them enter these. So he gave them permission. [33] Then the demons came out of the man and entered the pigs, and the herd rushed down the steep bank into the lake and drowned.

Did you hear it? It was much louder that time. But it hits the highest peak in an episode not long before Jesus is crucified in a city called Caesarea Philippi.

Pause to think about Matthew 16 for a minute. Stop to read it if you need to, but as you do, I need you to put yourself in the shoes of a first-century person. It's important to know the audience, and this audience would have accepted the next part without hesitation. You won't accept it as a modern scientifically minded reader, but it was accepted as simple truth by the original audience.

Caesarea Philippi is in the Northern parts of Israel at the base of the Bashan Mountain Range. At the foot of the mountains was a temple complex to the gods, not God, but to the pagan gods. At this place was a cave called the cave of Pan. Maybe you have heard of it. It was considered by the ancient world to be the Gates of Hell. The very place where one could access the underworld. It isn't a metaphor. This is what the audience that day believed. It is real to them.

Do you see why I asked you to put yourselves in the shoes of a first-century person? We are scientific, modern people, and we are above things like that. However, the original audience was not scientific. They thought differently than us, and I would argue, better than us when it comes to the Bible.

Standing at this spot, which happens to be a big rock (geologically speaking, literally a rock.), Jesus asked his disciples, "Who do people say that I am?"

We'll pick up in Verse 14.

> Matthew 16:14-18 ESV
>
> [14] And they said, "Some say John the Baptist, others say Elijah, and others Jeremiah or one of the prophets." [15] He said to them, "But who do you say that I am?" [16] Simon Peter replied, "You are the Christ, the Son of the living God." [17] And Jesus answered him, "Blessed are you, Simon Bar-Jonah! For flesh and blood has not revealed this to you, but my Father who is in heaven. [18] And I tell you, you are Peter, and on this rock, I will build my church, and the gates of hell shall not prevail against it."

A few of you will recognize a call-out when you hear one. You see, in most places, you don't go to someone's front door and say, "This is my house," unless you are prepared to make it your house. You see, the lion of the tribe of Judah, the strong arm of the Lord, went to the enemy's front door, slammed his fist against the door a few times, and let everyone know, "This is mine, and there ain't nothing you can do about it."

I know what you have been taught. I know Peter's name means, or sounds like, "stone" and some say that Peter was made the first Pope on that day, but I think we've missed it. Jesus went to the enemy's front door, to the Gates of Hell, to pick a fight, and he was successful. How do I know? Because in just a short time, he was dead.

You might think to yourself, "he should have learned to fight before he picked one." Well, he knew what he was doing. To prove it I want to take you to Revelation 1. Let me set this up.

John is on the island of Patmos, a Roman prison colony, exiled there because of the testimony of Jesus. He is in the spirit on the Lord's Day and has a vision. He sees Jesus as he is in Heaven and is given instructions to write.

From there, two passages stick out as they relate to what we have been talking about: The unseen realm and its real-world consequences.

In Verses 4 and 5, we read: This is John speaking:

> Revelation 1:4-5
>
> [4] Grace to you and peace from him who is and who was and who is to come, and from the seven spirits who are before his throne, [5] and from Jesus Christ the faithful witness, the firstborn of the dead, and the ruler of kings on earth.

I want to emphasize "ruler of kings on earth." This is John's way of describing who he is seeing. John tells us, "Greetings from the ruler of the kings on earth."

Remember what Jesus said? "Since John, the kingdom is coming violently, and the violent take it by force." What we see on the cross is an act of violence against Jesus, but it was a strategic move that put him in the place to do what comes next.

> Revelation 1:17-18
>
> [17] "...Fear not, I am the first and the last, [18] and the living one. I died, and behold, I am alive forevermore, and I have the keys of Death and Hades."

Jesus presents himself as the ruler of the kings on earth and as the one holding the keys belonging to Death and Hades. Apparently, Jesus can fight.

What the enemy thought was a death blow to God's plan to reestablish his kingdom was the final nail in their coffins. You see, when Jesus muttered, 'It is finished,' the rebellious host of heaven started rejoicing. They had finally won, but then there was this sound. It seemed far off in the distance at first, but it grew louder. What was it? What could it be? It sounded like the growl of a lion. When I think about it, I can sense the uneasy feeling that was spreading among the ranks. But before they could scout it out, the gates of the kingdom of hell were thrown open, and in walked the righteous one, the arm of God, the lion of the tribe of Judah. He was there to set things in order. It is important to remember what was said in Isaiah 24.

> Isaiah 24:21 ESV
>
> On that day, the LORD will punish the host of heaven, in heaven, and the kings of the earth, on the earth.

The plan to take back dominion was kept secret, and the cross was only the beginning. The enemy was unaware. They had played along to their own demise.

1 Corinthians 2:8 (ESV)

None of the rulers of this age understood this, for if they had, they would not have crucified the Lord of glory.

I want you to know that what the author of Isaiah prophesied was coming; John saw it in action. John saw it as it is still today. The kingdom of God has begun; it began when John the Baptist started paving the way with baptism for repentance. It was inaugurated on the cross and confirmed in the physical world by the resurrection.

John sees Jesus as the king of the earth, holding the keys to the enemy's castle. This is how we should see him too.

Earlier, we read Isaiah 51:9, *"Awake, awake, put on strength O arm of the Lord...* and in Psalm 82:8, we read, *"Arise O Lord and judge the earth, and inherit the nations."*

Both "awake" and "arise" can be translated from the Septuagint as *"resurrect!"* Resurrect, O Lord, and judge the earth and inherit the nations.

It was witnessed by Stephen as the crowd murdered him because of the testimony of Jesus.

Acts 7:55-56 ESV

[55] But he, full of the Holy Spirit, gazed into heaven and saw the glory of God, and Jesus standing at the right

hand of God. ⁵⁶ And he said, "Behold, I see the heavens opened, and the Son of Man standing at the right hand of God."

It was confirmed by Mark.

Mark 16:19 ESV

¹⁹ So then the Lord Jesus, after he had spoken to them, was taken up into heaven and sat down at the right hand of God.

And it was prophesied by Daniel.

Daniel 7:13-14

¹³ "I saw in the night visions,

and behold, with the clouds of heaven

there came one like a son of man,

and he came to the Ancient of Days

and was presented before him.

¹⁴ And to him was given dominion and glory and a kingdom, that all peoples, nations, and languages should serve him; his dominion is an everlasting dominion, which shall not pass away, and his kingdom one that shall not be destroyed."

See also: Romans 8:34; Ephesians 1:20; Colossians 3:1; Hebrews 1:3; 8:1; 10:12; 12:2; 1 Peter 3:22; Revelation 3:21; Matthew 22:44; Acts 2:33

Jesus reigns!

Let me help you out. Let me say out loud what you are thinking to yourself. It doesn't seem like it. Are you sure? Don't you think we have to wait for his return? First, I agree. It doesn't seem like a righteous king is on the throne of earth. Second, I do not think we have to wait for him to return. In fact, I think he is waiting for us to live in the realization of who sits on the throne. What began on the cross is in progress, and it is heading towards the conclusion described in Revelation 20:13-14.

> Revelation 20:13-14 ESV
>
> [13] And the sea gave up the dead who were in it, Death and Hades gave up the dead who were in them, and they were judged, each one of them, according to what they had done. [14] Then Death and Hades were thrown into the lake of fire. This is the second death, the lake of fire.

Paul said in 1 Corinthians 15:20-26 that Christ reigns, his resurrection proves it, and furthermore, he must continue *until all enemies are put under his feet.*

Did you catch that?

- **He must reign until...**

His reign has begun; he sits on the throne at the right hand of God, and his kingdom is in process. It is moving forward. The last of the enemies to be destroyed will be Death, but the first has long been locked up. It's an ongoing battle.

Jesus presents himself to John as the ruler of the kings on earth and as having the keys belonging to Death and Hades. He must reign until he has put all enemies under his feet. We live in the "until."

The questions we need to answer for ourselves are these:

- Is Jesus currently the ruler of the kings on earth?
- Does he currently hold the key belonging to Death and Hades?

I want to suggest to you that many believers will say yes to both questions but they live like the answer is no. I hope that this book will help change that. I have given you the scriptural foundation for living like the answers are yes.

Jesus currently reigns over the earth, and he currently holds the keys belonging to Death and Hades. I believe that the sooner the church starts living like it, the sooner we will see the conclusion we read about in Revelation. Death will be dealt with, and heaven will come to earth. Hopefully, you haven't forgotten, that is the goal. *"Your kingdom come, your will be done, on earth as it is in heaven."* (Matthew 6:10)

If it seems I'm implying that believers can participate in the return of Christ, I am. I don't have time for them here, but you should read Matthew 23:39 and see how Jesus ties his return to his chosen people, Israel, accepting their Messiah. Read Romans 11:11-15 where Paul says resurrection depends on Israel accepting their Messiah. Furthermore, and especially, read 2 Peter 3:11-15. This one I will add.

> 2 Peter 3:11-15 ESV
>
> [11] Since all these things are thus to be dissolved, what sort of people ought you to be in lives of holiness and godliness, [12] waiting for and hastening the coming of the day of God, because of which the heavens will be set on fire and dissolved, and the heavenly bodies will melt as they burn! [13] But according to his promise we are waiting for new heavens and a new earth in which righteousness dwells. [14] Therefore, beloved, since you are waiting for these, be diligent to be found by him without spot or blemish, and at peace. [15] And count the patience of our Lord as salvation, just as our beloved brother Paul also wrote to you according to the wisdom given him....

Here Peter gives us language from the Revelation by saying the heavens will be set on fire and dissolved, and the heavenly bodies will melt as they burn. Maybe you are beginning to see that language in a different light, a light that exposes the unseen realm.

Peter encourages the believers to live holy lives as they wait for and hasten the day of God. The word hasten means to *"cause something to happen by exercising special effort."*[2] In what way are we to exercise special effort? Peter says, "Count the patience of our Lord as salvation." He simply means that every day the Lord gives us before he returns is a day to spread his kingdom. If you want to hasten the day of the Lord, share the gospel, and participate in the great commission. Furthermore, live kingdom lives that witness to others that you believe your king is on the throne. Be charitable, live in love and live holy.

---

[2] **"to cause someth. to happen or come into being by exercising special effort, *hasten"*** William Arndt et al., *A Greek-English Lexicon of the New Testament and Other Early Christian Literature* (Chicago: University of Chicago Press, 2000), 938.

The Deuteronomy 32 Worldview

The Deuteronomy 32 worldview is the idea that the God of Israel, at the Tower of Babel event, divided up the people, creating nations, and placed over those nations lesser gods called the sons of God, but Israel he kept for himself, as Deuteronomy 32:8-9 tells us.

> Deuteronomy 32:8-9
>
> [8] When the Most High gave to the nations their inheritance, when he divided mankind, he fixed the borders of the peoples according to the number of the sons of God.
>
> [9] But the LORD's portion is his people, Jacob his allotted heritage.

The foundation for Deuteronomy 32:8-9 is Genesis 11, the story of the Tower of Babel. Genesis 11:1-9 tells us that the people disobeyed God's command to spread out. Instead, they gathered in a place called the plain of Shinar and began to build a city and a tower which would have a top in the heavens. God saw that they disobeyed his command to spread out, and his solution was to confuse their languages causing them to spread out according to languages. This is how God divided mankind.

Dividing mankind, he created borders and gave to each of these new nations vassal kings. These were members of his divine council who would rule over them and report back on the state of their dominions. Deuteronomy 32:8 calls these vassal kings, sons of God.

Paul talks about these borders in Acts 17.

Acts 17:24-27

[24] The God who made the world and everything in it, being Lord of heaven and earth, does not live in temples made by man, [25] nor is he served by human hands, as though he needed anything, since he himself gives to all mankind life and breath and everything. [26] **And he made from one man every nation of mankind to live on all the face of the earth, having determined allotted periods and the boundaries of their dwelling place,** [27] that they should seek God, and perhaps feel their way toward him and find him.

Paul is echoing a verse from Job.

Job 12:23

He makes nations great, and destroys them; He enlarges nations, and guides them.

Furthermore, Paul acknowledges these powers, these vassal kings, in several places.

Ephesians 6:11-12

¹¹ Put on the whole armor of God, that you may be able to stand against the wiles of the devil. ¹² **For we do not wrestle against flesh and blood, but against principalities, against powers, against the rulers of the darkness of this age, against spiritual *hosts* of wickedness in the heavenly *places*.**

Colossians 1:16

¹⁶ For by Him all things were created that are in heaven and that are on earth, visible and invisible, whether thrones or dominions or principalities or powers.

Ephesians 1:20-21

He raised Him from the dead and seated *Him* at His right hand in the heavenly *places*, ²¹ far above all principality and power and might and dominion, and every name that is named, not only in this age but also in that which is to come.

Paul has not made this up, he is sharing with us ideas that come from Old Testament Passages like Daniel 10.

Daniel 10 tells the story of a spiritual being called the Prince of Persia who disrupts a heavenly message on its way to Daniel. For three weeks, the Prince of Persia withstood the messenger until the prince of Israel, the angel Michael, shows up to help. For 21 days, Daniel has prayed and fasted when this heavenly messenger shows up. When he does, he tells Daniel...

> Daniel 10:12-13
>
> "Do not fear, Daniel, for from the first day that you set your heart to understand, and to humble yourself before your God, your words were heard; , and I have come because of your words. [13] But the prince of the kingdom of Persia withstood me twenty-one days; and behold, Michael, one of the chief princes, came to help me, for I had been left alone there with the kings of Persia.

A few verses later, the angel leaves, but before he goes, he says,

> "And now I must return to fight with the prince of Persia; , and when I have gone forth, indeed, the prince of Greece will come. [21] But I will tell you what is noted in the Scripture of Truth. (No one upholds me against these, except Michael, your prince." (Daniel 10:20-21)

Daniel 10 gives us a picture of the heavenly rulers (the invisible powers) that Deuteronomy 32:8 was referring to, specifically, the kings of Persia, the Prince of Persia, and the Prince of Greece. These are all examples of the sons of God from Deuteronomy 32.

Maybe you are reading your Bible and Deuteronomy 32:8 doesn't say "sons of god" but instead, "sons of Israel." Many versions do. I often use the NKJV in my Bible studies, and the NKJV reads, "sons of Israel." How are we to deal with this difference? What makes one right and the other wrong? That's a legitimate question and there are several ways to deal with it, but I will focus on just two reasons for accepting "sons of God" as the correct translation.

First, Israel was not a nation at the time of the Tower of Babel nor immediately after. It isn't until after the Tower incident that God calls Abraham to be the father of his chosen people. There are no sons of Israel to rule over the nations created at Babel, nor have they ever ruled over the nations. In fact, the nations have raged against them.

Second, and I think most convincing, is the way the NKJV and other translations deal with other verses with similar implications to Deuteronomy 32:8. From the same chapter, the NKJV acknowledges these powers and calls them foreign gods:

> Deuteronomy 32:16-17 NKJV
>
> [16] They provoked Him to jealousy with foreign *gods*; With abominations, they provoked Him to anger. [17] They sacrificed to demons, not to God, *To gods* they did not

know, To new *gods,* new arrivals That your fathers did not fear.

In Deuteronomy chapter 4, The NKJV acknowledges that other powers, called the host of heaven, were given to the people of the earth while God chose Israel.

Deuteronomy 4:19-20 NKJV

[19] And *take heed,* lest you lift your eyes to heaven, and *when* you see the sun, the moon, and the stars, all the host of heaven, you feel driven to worship them and serve them, which the LORD your God has given to all the peoples under the whole heaven as a heritage. [20] But the LORD has taken you and brought you out of the iron furnace, out of Egypt, to be His people, an inheritance, as you are this day.

God, Yahweh, has given the host of heaven to the nations for them to worship, but Israel he has kept for his own. The host of heaven are the vassal kings we spoke of earlier, of which the princes of Persia and Greece are examples.

God warns his people not to worship these powers. From the NKJV, we read:

Deuteronomy 17:2-5 NKJV

[2] "If there is found among you, within any of your gates which the LORD your God gives you, a man or a woman

who has been wicked in the sight of the LORD your God, in transgressing His covenant, ³ who has gone and served other gods and worshiped them, either the sun or moon or any of the host of heaven, which I have not commanded, ⁴ and it is told you, and you hear *of it,* then you shall inquire diligently. And if *it is* indeed true *and* certain that such an abomination has been committed in Israel, ⁵ then you shall bring out to your gates that man or woman who has committed that wicked thing, and shall stone to death that man or woman with stones.

And again, Deuteronomy tells us that there were gods that were not given to Israel.

Deuteronomy 29:24-26 NKJV

'Why has the LORD done so to this land? What does the heat of this great anger mean?" ²⁵ Then *people* would say: 'Because they have forsaken the covenant of the LORD God of their fathers, which He made with them when He brought them out of the land of Egypt; ²⁶ for they went and served other gods and worshiped them, gods that they did not know and that He had not given to them.'

You can see that in other passages, the NKJV acknowledges these powers, these vassal kings that were given to the other nations to rule over them.

The book of Job acknowledges these sons of God and that they appear before him to report.

> Job 1:6-7
>
> [6] Now, there was a day when the sons of God came to present themselves before the LORD, and Satan also came among them. [7] And the LORD said to Satan, "From where do you come?" So Satan answered the LORD and said, "From going to and fro on the earth, and from walking back and forth on it."

And again, in Chapter 2.

> Job 2:1-2
>
> Again there was a day when the sons of God came to present themselves before the LORD, and Satan came also among them to present himself before the LORD. [2] And the LORD said to Satan, "From where do you come?" Satan answered the LORD and said, "From going to and fro on the earth, and from walking back and forth on it."

I believe we can connect these sons of God in Job to the sons of God in Deuteronomy 32. They are likely reporting to God their work and the status of the lands given to them.

King David acknowledges the borders and the gods that are put over the foreign nations. In 1 Samuel 26, we find David on the run from King Saul. King Saul is in the wilderness seeking to kill David when he gets really close without knowing it. He gets so close that his own life would have been in danger had it not been for the integrity of David, who was close enough to kill him with his sword. Later, seeking an opportunity to end the conflict, David shouts down to Saul...

> 1 Samuel 26:17-19
>
> [17] Then Saul knew David's voice, and said, "*Is* that your voice, my son David?" David said, "*It is* my voice, my lord, O king." [18] And he said, "Why does my lord thus pursue his servant? For what have I done, or what evil *is* in my hand? [19] Now therefore, please, let my lord the king hear the words of his servant: If the LORD has stirred you up against me, let Him accept an offering. But if *it is* the children of men, *may* they *be* cursed before the LORD, for they have driven me out this day from sharing in the inheritance of the LORD, saying, 'Go, serve other gods.'

David clearly connects being driven from the land with serving other gods. He realizes what Deuteronomy teaches us. The other lands have been put under the direction of lesser beings appointed by the God of Israel. For David, being forced into other lands is to be forced to worship other gods. There is a very real connection between the borders spoken of by Paul in Acts 17 and this passage from 1 Samuel.

There is another passage that shows us the importance of the borders. It comes from the story of Naaman, the commander of the Syrian army. Naaman was a leper. In Naaman's house was a Hebrew girl who told Naaman's wife about the prophet Elisha. She says, *"Would that my Lord were with the prophet who is in Samaria! He would cure him of his leprosy."* Naaman goes to see the prophet, and the prophet tells him to go dip in the river Jordan seven times, something Naaman refuses to do until he is encouraged by his servants to at least try it. When he does, he is healed. Naaman, wanting to show gratitude and deliver due payment, comes to Elisha and offers a gift, but Elisha refuses the gift. Naaman insists at first, but the prophet will not budge. Then Naaman makes a very odd request:

> 2 Kings 5:17
>
> Then Naaman said, "If not, please let there be given to your servant two mule loads of earth, for from now on

your servant will not offer burnt offering or sacrifice to any god but the LORD.

Why is he asking for two mule loads of dirt from Israel? Because Naaman understands cosmic geography as it is called. He understands that the God of Israel, though powerful enough to heal leprosy, is not the God of his homeland, Syria. He also understands, like David, that to worship God, or a god, properly, you should be in the land that belongs to that god. It is proper to worship the God of Israel in Israel but not elsewhere. The other gods will be angry. Naaman seeks a clever remedy. His request tells us that he is going home to build an altar to the God of Israel on ground from Israel. He says, *"From now on, your servant will not offer burnt offering or sacrifice to any god but the Lord."* Furthermore, because part of his job was to escort the king of Syria into the house of Rimmon, the Syrian god, he asks the prophet to seek God's pardon on his behalf for doing such a thing. Elisha says, *"Go in peace."*

Naaman understands that to properly worship God, he needs to be on the land from Israel, so he takes dirt home with him.

Let's look at a few more passages that inform this perspective of lesser gods being over the nations.

Concerning Egypt

Jeremiah 46:25

The L ORD of hosts, the God of Israel, said: "Behold, I am bringing punishment upon Amon of Thebes, and Pharaoh and Egypt **and her gods** and her kings, upon Pharaoh and those who trust in him.

Concerning Moab

Jeremiah 48:7

For, because you trusted in your works and your treasures, you also shall be taken, and **Chemosh** shall go into exile with his priests and his officials. Chemosh is the god of Moab and one of the gods Solomon built a temple for in Israel.

Concerning Ammon (the Ammonites)

Jeremiah 49:3

...For Milcom shall go into exile, with his priests and his officials. Milcom is the god of the Ammonites Concerning Damascus.

Jeremiah 49:27

And I will kindle a fire in the wall of Damascus, and it shall devour the strongholds of Ben-hadad."Ben Hadad is the ruler in Damascus and his name means "son of Adad". Adad was the god of thunder and storm.

Concerning Babylon

Jeremiah 50:2

Babylon is taken, **Bel** is put to shame, **Merodach** is dismayed. Her images are put to shame, her idols are dismayed.'

Both Bel and Merodach are names for the god of Babylon referred to as Marduk.

When God judges the nations, he is judging the gods of those nations, even primarily the gods of the nations. Here is what I am suggesting and the point I hope you take away from this. Paul tells us that we do not wrestle against flesh and blood but against powers and principalities. I want to suggest to you that, like us, God does not wrestle directly with flesh and blood. His enemies are the spiritual enemies that rebelled against him and did not rule as he had directed. This is the primary story of John's Revelation.

The Host Of Heaven
The Sun, Moon, and Stars as Divine Beings

When considering many of the passages in the Bible where the author uses language concerning the sun, moon, mountains, and stars, we must force our modern and scientific minds to consider the culture and belief system of the author and his original audience. We must ask ourselves if we are assigning a modern understanding to passages that have a very different point of view. A Google search for *"What is a star?"* will quickly give us, *"A star is an astronomical object comprising a luminous spheroid of plasma held together by its gravity."*[3] It is nearly impossible for the modern mind to forget that definition when we read a passage like Revelation 8:10, *"The third angel blew his trumpet, and a great star fell from heaven."* (See also Is. 13:10, 34:2-4) Almost impossible is not impossible, especially when we commit to understanding that the Bible meant something to its original audience. It made sense to them. A Google search for *"What is a star?"* in the mid-first century would have returned something like, "A star is a divine being who affects the destinies of men on earth. Deities worthy of worship."

---

[3] https://en.wikipedia.org/wiki/Star

There are two scenes in Disney's Lion King (1994) that illustrate this point perfectly. The first is found early in the movie where Mufasa is explaining the stars to his cub, Simba. He says, *"Look at the stars. The great kings of the past look down on us from those stars." "Really?"* Simba asks. *"Yes. So, whenever you feel alone, just remember that those kings will always be there to guide you. And so will I."* Later in the movie, when Simba is all grown up, he, Pumba, and Timone are laying in the field when Pumba asks, *"Timone, ever wonder what those sparkling darts are up there?"* Timone answers, *"I don't wonder, I know. They are fireflies..."* To which Pumba answers, *"Oh. Geez. I always thought they were balls of gas burning billions of miles away."* To which Timone answers, *"Pumba, to you, everything is gas."*

These two scenes help us understand passages like Revelation 8 and 9. We are Pumba. To us, everything is gas, I mean, scientific. Stars are big balls of gas burning billions of miles away. Mountains that fall from the sky are asteroids or comets. The events we see in Revelation, like the sun, moon, and stars going dark are obviously from the dust cloud created by a large meteor impact, or eclipses. But I believe the modern reader too quickly imposes their definitions onto the words of the biblical authors. We fail to consider that they sometimes have different definitions for common words. To John, the stars are not big balls of gas burning billions of miles away; they are divine beings worshiped by the people. They are called "the host of heaven" and God warns his people, Israel, not to worship them.

Deuteronomy 17:2-3

² "If there is found among you, within any of your towns that the LORD your God is giving you, a man or woman who does what is evil in the sight of the LORD your God, in transgressing his covenant, ³ **and has gone and served other gods and worshiped them, or the sun or the moon or any of the host of heaven**, which I have forbidden...

Deuteronomy 4:19

And beware **lest you raise your eyes to heaven, and when you see the sun and the moon and the stars, all the host of heaven, you be drawn away and bow down to them and serve them**, things that the LORD your God has allotted to all the peoples under the whole heaven.

In both passages, we see the sun, moon, and stars called "the host of heaven" and the people of God are told not to worship them. But they do not listen.

2 Kings 17:16

> And they abandoned all the commandments of the LORD their God, and made for themselves metal images of two calves, and they made an Asherah and **worshiped all the host of heaven** and served Baal.

2 Kings 21:3

> For he rebuilt the high places that Hezekiah his father had destroyed, and he erected altars for Baal and made an Asherah, as Ahab king of Israel had done, and **worshiped all the host of heaven and served them.**

King Josiah made it right for a time, removing all the idols of worship.

2 Kings 23:5

> [5] And he deposed the priests whom the kings of Judah had ordained to make offerings in the high places at the cities of Judah and around Jerusalem; **those also who burned incense to Baal, to the sun and the moon and the constellations and all the host of the heavens.**

In Psalm 148:2-3, the angels, his host, and the sun, moon, and stars are told to praise the Lord.

In Zephaniah 1:1-5 God promises to judge those who have bowed down on the roofs to the host of heaven and their king, Milcom, a god of the Ammonites. His name is sometimes associated with El (most high) or Molech. These are gods from other nations the Israelites imported. And in Isaiah 24:21-23 we see that God will judge the fallen host of heaven and he associates them with the sun and the moon.

Isaiah 24:21-23

[21] On that day, **the LORD will punish the host of heaven, in heaven**, and the kings of the earth, on the earth. [22] They will be gathered together as prisoners in a pit; they will be shut up in a prison, and after many days, they will be punished. [23] **Then the moon will be confounded and the sun ashamed, for the LORD of hosts reigns** on Mount Zion and in Jerusalem, and his glory will be before his elders.

It is clear from scripture that the sun, moon, and stars are called and numbered among the host of heaven, and they are the gods given to the nations as an inheritance in Deuteronomy 32:8. This is the mind of John as he writes Revelation 8-9. That the host of heaven are more than just twinkling lights in the sky is attested by 1 Kings 22:1-28 where the prophet Micaiah has a vision and, in his vision, he sees the Lord sitting on his throne and all the host of heaven standing beside him on his right and on his left. In verse 20, God speaks to the host of heaven, and they answer him. This is the passage that helps us truly accept the idea of God's council. It becomes something we can visualize.

John himself lets the modern readers in on the secret. In Revelation 9:1, he sees a star fall from heaven, and the star is given a key. In Revelation 12, we read a passage that many are familiar with, but few take the time to look at for themselves. Many believers are familiar with the idea that Satan deceived a third of the angels, but the Bible doesn't say that. This is what it says...

> Revelation 12:3-4
>
> [3] And another sign appeared in heaven: behold, a great red dragon, with seven heads and ten horns, and on his heads seven diadems. [4] His tail swept down a third of the stars of heaven and cast them to the earth.

This is not the place to debate the meaning and timing of this verse, but it does illustrate my point well. What we know from tradition as a third of the angels falling, John describes as a third of the stars. Satan brings down a third of the stars, not angels, but that's because, to John, there is no difference. When the original audience heard Revelation 8-9, they didn't think of comets, asteroids, meteors, and certainly not nuclear war; they would have pulled from the same knowledge base as the author, their first-century understanding of the host of heaven. They would have known John meant divine beings.

The book of Enoch, written as early as 200 BC but known to the biblical authors and quoted by Jude and Peter, says this...

Enoch 21

21.1 And I proceeded to where things were chaotic. 2 And I saw there something horrible: I saw neither a heaven above nor a firmly founded earth, but a place chaotic and horrible. 3 And there I saw seven stars of the heaven bound together in it, like great mountains and burning with fire. 4 Then I said: 'For what sin are they bound, and on what account have they been cast in hither?' 5 Then said Uriel, one of the holy angels, who was with me, and was chief over them, and said: 'Enoch, why dost thou ask, and why art thou eager for the truth? 6 These are of the number of the stars of heaven which have transgressed the commandment of the Lord, and are bound here till ten thousand years, the time entailed by their sins, are consummated.'

Let me say this before moving on, a book that is not divinely inspired does not mean "not important."

Consider Isaiah 24:21-22 from above. Verse 22 says concerning the kings of earth and the host of heaven, *"They will be gathered together as prisoners in a pit, they will be shut up in a prison, and after many days they will be punished."*

Both Revelation 9 and 20 talk about a pit where demons and Satan are locked away. I believe this is Sheol or Hades.

These are the things in the mind of the original audience, and they would have understood John far better than we do.

The Language of the Past

The language of Revelation is not new to the original audience. These aren't previously unknown ideas that John has received about future cataclysmic warfare. This is language from their scriptures and their cultures. This is how God describes what will happen to Edom when he judges them for helping Babylon who went beyond what God sent them to do.

> Isaiah 34:1-5
>
> [1] Draw near, O nations, to hear, and give attention, O peoples! Let the earth hear, and all that fills it; the world and all that comes from it.
>
> [2] For the LORD is enraged against all the nations, and furious against **all their host**; he has devoted them to destruction, has given them over for slaughter.
>
> [3] Their slain shall be cast out, and the stench of their corpses shall rise; the mountains shall flow with their blood.

⁴ All the host of heaven shall rot away, and the skies roll up like a scroll. All their host shall fall, as leaves fall from the vine, like leaves falling from the fig tree.

⁵ For my sword has drunk its fill **in the heavens**; behold, it descends for judgment upon Edom, upon the people I have devoted to destruction. In verse 9 and 10, we read...

⁹ And the streams of Edom shall be turned into pitch, and her soil into sulfur; her land shall become burning pitch.

¹⁰ Night and day, it shall not be quenched; its smoke shall go up forever. From generation to generation, it shall lie waste; none shall pass through it forever and ever.

This is language very similar to what we find in Revelation 8-9, but there was no nuclear war nor were the skies rolled away and its star shaken from it when Edom was judged. What we see is that God's sword first took vengeance in the heavens before the physical manifestations of it were seen on earth in Edom.

Before this, God tells us what he will do to Babylon for going beyond what he sent them to do.

Isaiah 13:9-13

⁹ Behold, the day of the Lord comes, cruel, with wrath and fierce anger, to make the land a desolation and to destroy its sinners from it.

¹⁰ For the stars of the heavens and their constellations will not give their light; the sun will be dark at its rising, and the moon will not shed its light.

¹¹ I will punish the world for its evil, and the wicked for their iniquity; I will put an end to the pomp of the arrogant, and lay low the pompous pride of the ruthless.

¹² I will make people more rare than fine gold, and mankind than the gold of Ophir.

¹³ Therefore I will make the heavens tremble, and the earth will be shaken out of its place, at the wrath of the Lord of hosts in the day of his fierce anger.

Like Edom, Babylon was judged but without nuclear weapons and without the end of creation, which is what would happen if the language was about physical creation and not language that told us how God was judging the host of heaven over Edom and Babylon. Here's the point: If the heavens were shaken and the earth shaken from its place when God judged Babylon, we would not be here today. It isn't language about the physical world only. Isaiah is telling us that God judged the fallen sons of God over Edom and Babylon. God judges the host of heaven first. (Refer to Daniel 10 where the Prince of Persia was removed by angels before the prince of Greece came in. Historically, we know Greece defeated Persia.)

Furthermore, many of the things described in the Revelation happened in Egypt. The destruction was brought against Egypt not by an invading army, and certainly not nuclear war. Destruction was brought the hand of God, and he used angels to do it.

Psalm 78:42-51

[42] They did not remember his power or the day when he redeemed them from the foe,

[43] when he performed his signs in Egypt and his marvels in the fields of Zoan.

[44] He turned their rivers to blood, so that they could not drink of their streams.

[45] He sent among them swarms of flies, which devoured them, and frogs, which destroyed them.

[46] He gave their crops to the destroying locust and the fruit of their labor to the locust.

[47] He destroyed their vines with hail and their sycamores with frost.

⁴⁸ He gave over their cattle to the hail and their flocks to thunderbolts.

⁴⁹ He let loose on them his burning anger, wrath, indignation, and distress, **a company of destroying angels**.

⁵⁰ He made a path for his anger; he did not spare them from death, but gave their lives over to the plague.

⁵¹ He struck down every firstborn in Egypt, the firstfruits of their strength in the tents of Ham.

Verse 49 says God *let loose on them his burning anger, wrath, indignation, and distress by a company of destroying angels.* In the Septuagint, they are called *"evil angels."* Why do we insist on a literal interpretation, or an interpretation that requires modern nuclear warfare, to explain what we read in the Revelation when God did the same things in Egypt, Assyria, Babylon, and Edom without cataclysmic destruction and nuclear warfare?

In Chapter 11, we are told the two witnesses have the power to shut the sky, that no rain may fall during the days of their prophesying, and they have power over the waters to turn them into blood and to strike the earth with every kind of plague, as often as they desire. When we have an example such as Egypt, where no warfare was involved but similar things happened, or an example such as the prophet Elijah who prophesied there would be no rain and there was no rain, why do we insist on taking the supernatural out of Revelation leaning only on modern scientific reasoning like meteors, asteroids, and nuclear warfare. The original audience would not have done that.

I am not promising that there will never be a nuclear war. Nor am I saying that God will not use catastrophes from heaven, like a large asteroid impact, to judge the world. What I am saying is that the language that makes us think those things is clearly tied to divine beings in God's word and the culture from which it comes. That makes me think we should look there first to understand what John is saying.

Do not take what I have said in this chapter as a promise that there will be no warfare nor natural catastrophes. I've said in other places that the Prince of Persia being deposed by the angels of heaven and replaced by the Prince of Greece played out historically. Greece defeated Persia. War will take place in what is our natural world. What I am saying is that the language we use to talk about war and natural catastrophes is the language referring to the fallen host of heaven (the fallen sons of God). God will remove the stars, darken the sun, shake the mountains, but they are exactly what John and the prophets meant them to be: the rebellious members of the unseen realm. They are the powers, principalities, thrones, and dominions Paul calls our enemies. By focusing on the natural, we miss the point of the Bible and the cross. God has rebellious sons that he is dealing with, and the cross was part of it.

Colossians 2:13-15

¹³ And you, who were dead in your trespasses and the uncircumcision of your flesh, God made alive together with him, having forgiven us all our trespasses, ¹⁴ by canceling the record of debt that stood against us with its legal demands. This he set aside, nailing it to the cross. ¹⁵ He disarmed the rulers and authorities and put them to open shame, by triumphing over them in him.

I'll close this chapter with a relevant passage from Joel 2:28-32...

"'And in the last days it shall be, God declares, that I will pour out my Spirit on all flesh, and your sons and your daughters shall prophesy, and your young men shall see visions, and your old men shall dream dreams; even on my male servants and female servants in those days I will pour out my Spirit, and they shall prophesy. And I will show wonders in the heavens above and signs on the earth below, blood, and fire, and vapor of smoke; the sun shall be turned to darkness and the moon to blood, before the day of the Lord comes, the great and magnificent day.

And it shall come to pass that everyone who calls upon the name of the Lord shall be saved.'" [4]

If you follow anyone who talks about end-time events on a regular basis, you've heard Joel 2:28-32 discussed as an end times event. Even if you don't follow those things, you've heard people talk about things like blood moons and eclipses. Many in the church make a big deal about them every time we experience one.

But what I read to you was not Joel 2; it was Peter quoting Joel 2 in Acts. 2:17-21. And Peter begins like this, *"For these people are not drunk as you suppose, since it is only the third hour of the day. But this is what was uttered through the prophet Joel."* (Acts 2:15-16)

What we are waiting for might not be as we were told. Instead, it has been happening since the days of John the Baptist when he preached the coming Messiah was here; it's not all out in the future. The Kingdom of God is going forth violently (Matthew 11:12). The kingdom is taking ground with the gospel, and the stars are falling by way of the powers, the rebellious host of heaven He is defeating.

---

[4] *The Holy Bible: English Standard Version* (Wheaton, IL: Crossway Bibles, 2016), Ac 2:17–21.

The cross was about erasing borders, specifically cosmic borders. The sons of God were stripped from their posts. They are being deposed, and in their place is king Jesus. He must reign until all enemies are placed under his feet. The last enemy to be defeated will be Death (1 Corinthians 15:20-28). When that is accomplished, he will hand it all over to God. You can read about it in Revelation 20-22.

Applying What We've Learned

Over the last few chapters, we've learned that God divided the nations and confused their languages at the Tower of Babel event and God chose to rule over the nations via government. He set over them the sons of God, Deuteronomy 32:8. But he kept for himself Jacob, or Israel, by choosing from among the nations one man to father that nation, Abraham. We learned the sons of God who were placed over the nations did not rule as God commanded. They took advantage of mankind and ruled wickedly. They accepted worship and did not point mankind back to God (Yahweh) who created them, the God of Heaven, the God of Israel. Their punishment? *"You will die like men"* Psalm 82:7. Jesus' birth, the ministry of John the Baptist, and especially the cross were all part of the kingdom of God coming to earth to undo what the fallen elohim, the sons of God, had gotten wrong. Jesus came to restore God's plan for Earth, and the first order of business was, and still is, to judge the host of heaven, described as the sun, moon, stars, and other things, that stand opposed to the plan. We will continue that story now.

By this point, we should have a pretty good grip on the unseen realm and John's use of it. In this chapter, we will begin to apply it. That being the case, we will focus mainly on

Revelation Chapter 6, but first, let's highlight the first Five chapters.

Chapter 1: John sees Jesus as he is today, in heaven, reigning as king over the earth and the churches. He is glorified and holds the keys that once belonged to Death and Hades. In the second chapter of this book, we learned that this is present and ongoing. This is how Jesus is today. JESUS REIGNS! He sits at the right hand of God, and he is the son of man from Daniel 7 who is currently waging war on his enemies. 1 Corinthians 15:25 says, *"He must reign UNTIL all his enemies have been put under his feet"*.

Chapters 2-3: The letters to the seven churches of Revelation. We won't spend any time in Chapters 2 and 3, but I want to point out that these were seven real churches in Asia Minor. While they are sometimes seen as representing church ages, we shouldn't forget that they were real churches full of believers like churches today. I believe they are representative of all churches throughout the church age. We can learn from the encouragement and rebukes given to them.

Chapters 4-5: This is a heavenly scene. God is on his throne. It is like the other heavenly throne room scenes we have referenced from Isaiah 6 and Daniel 7. This one outlined in Chapters 4 and 5, is like Daniel 7 in that It's presented as a courtroom. God is on his throne, and he is the judge. But first...

Revelation 4:1 (ESV)

"After this, I looked, and behold, a door standing open in heaven! And the first voice, which I had heard speaking to me like a trumpet, said, 'Come up here, and I will show you what must take place after this.'"

This verse is important if we are to understand what John is writing. One of our rules is applicable here. John has a heavenly perspective. He has been invited into the unseen realm. Most of what John presents will only be understood if we understand the unseen realm and understand that it is his primary perspective throughout the book. That's why we have spent the first few chapters talking so much about it. There are heavenly hosts to judge, and John was allowed to see it from God's vantage point and he is told to record it for us.

There is a lot to notice in Chapters 4 and 5, but time prevents us from covering it all, so I will focus on something I think is important and recurring. Something we will see again in Chapter 6 and something I pointed out in previous sessions from the Old Testament. Do you remember our second Rule to understand the Revelation? It's the importance of the Old Testament.

The Four Creatures

Revelation 4:6-8 ESV

> ⁶ And before the throne, there was, as it were, a sea of glass, like crystal. And around the throne, on each side of the throne, are four living creatures, full of eyes in front and behind: ⁷ the first living creature like a lion, the second living creature like an ox, the third living creature with the face of a man, and the fourth living creature like an eagle in flight. ⁸ And the four living creatures, each of them with six wings, are full of eyes all around and within...

These are like the four creatures described for us by the prophet in Ezekiel Chapters 1 and 10. There are a few differences, but scholars are sure these are the same creatures or, at the least, the same type of creatures. We looked at these in Chapter 1, so just briefly...

Ezekiel says in 1:5, *"And from the midst of it came the likeness of four living creatures..."* In Verse 10, he writes, *"As for the likeness of their faces, each had a human face. The four had the face of a lion on the right side, the four had the face of an ox on the left side, and the four had the face of an eagle."*

Like I said, there are differences in the passages from Revelation and Ezekiel. John sees only one face per creature, while Ezekiel sees the creatures with four faces each, though the faces are the same. Another difference is found later in

Ezekiel 1:15-18 where the creatures have wheels. There are no wheels in Revelation 4.

Why the differences? Perspective, I suppose. In Ezekiel, the throne is not in Heaven; it is mobile. God, who is riding on his throne, has come to Ezekiel while John is invited into the throne room. In Ezekiel, the creatures are doing what they do: they carry the throne. God's throne is sometimes called the divine throne chariot because it moves. There are books written on the throne chariot, so we don't have time to explore it fully, but the creatures in Revelation are the same or of the same type as those in Ezekiel. They sometimes carry the throne of God, but in Revelation 4, they are resting.

I want to point out the eyes, along with the four faces of each creature, and the ease of their movement described by Ezekiel because I believe it becomes important in understanding what is being represented and that is, God is enthroned **on** the heavens. The creatures represent all of creation, not just created beings. All of it. God sits upon all of creation.

Psalm 103:19 ESV

[19] The LORD has established his throne in the heavens, and his kingdom rules over all.

In Hebrew, the preposition translated "in" can also be "on" or "upon"! The Lord has established his throne upon the heavens.

Isaiah 66:1 says, "Heaven is my throne." Jesus said in Matthew 5:34, "Do not take an oath at all, either by heaven, for it is the throne of God", adding, "or by the earth, for it is his footstool" (a quote from Is. 66:1).

> Matthew 23:22 ESV
>
> And whoever swears by heaven swears by the throne of God and by him who sits upon it.

Here's what I am suggesting: God is not enclosed by his creation. He is not out there in the heavens somewhere; he is upon it. God is not contained by his creation; he is outside of it. This is what the creatures communicate. Because they carry his throne, he is enthroned on them. He sits upon creation, which is what the creatures represent.

Their faces are the four directional points of the Mazzaroth (Hebrew for the Zodiac).

The Lion is Leo.
The Man is Aquarius.
The Bull is Taurus.

The Eagle is Scorpio, which has been presented as an eagle, a snake, or a scorpion, which is how we know it today.

The faces represent the four cardinal points or the four directions. The creatures move with ease and without turning. The eyes are the stars, like the eyes we see in the dark as a deer looks at us from the trees along the road at night; they look like stars in the night sky. The creatures communicate that God is enthroned on the heavens and sits in judgment over all creation. That's important because the readers from John's time believed the stars to be deities, especially the planets that moved through the night sky. They are the host of heaven. God is enthroned above the elohim whom he is about to judge and, sadly, those who worship the elohim.

These are the things we miss if we don't take time to understand the mind of the original reader. The Revelation has significance for us, but it had significance to its original audience as well, and they would need to understand it, and they did. I want to suggest to you that they understood it better than us because our modern scientific minds obscure the messaging.

The message the creatures present as they sit around the throne and as they carry the throne in Ezekiel is that God sits above all creation, even the other elohim, especially the elohim. It is a theological message that says, "Yahweh is the Most High."

For clarity, I do not promote astrology. It is demonic and a distraction from the real purpose of the heavens. Why look to the stars for guidance when we have access to the voice of the one who hung the stars and who sits upon them as his throne?

> Psalm 19:4 ESV
>
> The heavens declare the glory of God, and the sky above proclaims his handiwork.

That's what the creatures represent. God is Most High. He is enthroned above creation. All that we might choose to worship other than him sits beneath him. Amen? Amen.

Before moving on, I want to state that I believe the creatures are real. They exist. The fact that they represent something does not negate their existence.

In Chapter 5, a scroll is presented, and John laments the fact that no one has been found worthy to open it, but one of the elders from one of the 24 thrones says to John, *"Weep no more; behold, the Lion of the tribe of Judah, the Root of David, has conquered, so that he can open the scroll and its seven seals."* Then John sees a lamb standing as if it had been slain.

The lamb is the lion, and he is worthy to open the scroll, and so he does. We heard him growl in Chapter 2, but now it is time to hear him roar.

> Revelation 6:1-8 ESV

¹ Now I watched when the Lamb opened one of the seven seals, and I heard one of the four living creatures say with a voice like thunder, "Come!" ² And I looked, and behold, a white horse! And its rider had a bow, and a crown was given to him, and he came out conquering, and to conquer. ³ When he opened the second seal, I heard the second living creature say, "Come!" ⁴ And out came another horse, bright red. Its rider was permitted to take peace from the earth, so that people should slay one another, and he was given a great sword. ⁵ When he opened the third seal, I heard the third living creature say, "Come!" And I looked, and behold, a black horse! And its rider had a pair of scales in his hand. ⁶ And I heard what seemed to be a voice in the midst of the four living creatures, saying, "A quart of wheat for a denarius, and three quarts of barley for a denarius, and do not harm the oil and wine!" ⁷ When he opened the fourth seal, I heard the voice of the fourth living creature say, "Come!" ⁸ And I looked, and behold, a pale horse! And its rider's name was Death, and Hades followed him. And they were given authority over a fourth of the earth, to kill with sword and with famine and with pestilence and by wild beasts of the earth.

You see right away why we spent a few minutes focusing on the four creatures. They call forth the four horsemen. They are used to call them forth because they represent the four directions. These four horsemen come from and go into the four directions representing all creation. There is one who is clearly the leader, the rider on the white horse. He goes forth to conquer the earth. All of it.

Who is the rider on the White Horse?

There is some debate. Some see him as the antichrist who is in control of the other three, and all four represent evil. Others see him as Christ. The rider on the white horse from Revelation 19:11 is the one called *faithful and true*. That view presents a problem in the minds of some because clearly the rider on the white horse is the head of the other three. The destruction they bring comes because of the first rider's conquests. Some will have a hard time reconciling the idea that it is Jesus who brings the destruction of the other three horses.

What to do? What to do? Should we vote via survey? No. That wouldn't give us the truth. That would only give us a majority opinion," My thought is we do a bit of research. We could use the rules we were given in chapter one to determine if Jesus could be the rider on the white horse.

Remember the rules from the previous chapters. We've mentioned them already.

1. The Unseen Realm is real, and it matters if we are to understand what John is communicating.
2. John uses the Old Testament and what he uses and how he uses it matters if we are to understand the vision.

Number one seems obvious by now. We've determined that an unseen realm exists. It is the world in which the spiritual beings live, and it is John's current perspective, having been invited into Heaven and the unseen realm in Revelation 4:1. The four horsemen John sees are spiritual beings in the unseen realm.

Our second rule is to consider what the Old Testament might say about what is happening. Does the Old Testament inform us about this passage?

Yes. Along with what we have learned about the unseen realm.

The 4 Horsemen in the Old Testament and the Unseen Realm

Horsemen are described in Zechariah 1:7-17 where we are told they answer to the angel of the Lord. Their job is to patrol the earth and report. They are similar in color to the horsemen in the Revelation. Zechariah's horsemen report the whole world remains at rest. That sounds like a good thing, but it isn't to the Lord. Israel has been judged and exiled. The nations went too far in their judgment, and it angers God that his people are scattered, but the rest of the world is at rest.

The timing of Zechariah is just prior to the rebuilding of the temple. Solomon's temple was destroyed by the Babylonians, and in Zechariah, a remnant has returned to rebuild Jerusalem and the Temple.

The horsemen are mentioned again in Zechariah 6, this time as chariot teams of horses.

Zechariah 6:1-5 ESV

> [1] Again, I lifted my eyes and saw, and behold, four chariots came out from between two mountains. And the mountains were mountains of bronze. [2] The first chariot had red horses, the second black horses, [3] the third white horses, and the fourth chariot dappled horses—all of them strong. [4] Then I answered and said to the angel who talked with me, "What are these, my lord?" [5] And the angel answered and said to me, "These are going out to the four winds of heaven after presenting themselves before the Lord of all the earth."

Remember the creatures? They represent the four directions and tell us that God is sovereign over all creation. They tell us that God sits upon the heavens and here we see that his horsemen go out to the four winds of heaven. The four winds are the same as the four corners. God's rule is complete and there isn't a single square inch in the cosmos that won't bend to his will.

Zechariah tells us he saw these things in the night, meaning a night vision, a dream. His eyes are opened to the unseen realm. He has been invited, like John, to see the events of the unseen realm take place before they are realized in the natural world. What we see in Revelation 6 has an Old Testament precedent in Zechariah 1 and 6, and they, too, are given from the perspective of the spiritual world, the unseen realm. The Angel of the Lord, the rider on the white horse, commands spiritual horsemen.

Let's go a bit further.

In Revelation we read, *"And they were given authority over a fourth of the earth, to kill with sword and with famine and with pestilence and by wild beasts of the earth."* (Revelation 6:8)

"They" are the second, third, and fourth horsemen. "They together kill with sword, with famine, with pestilence, and by a wild beast." And "they" are driven by the first horsemen on the white horse. They are called forth by the creatures that surround God's throne representing the conquest as covering all creation. Their four instruments of destruction are promised curses in the Old Testament.

Let me show you. Speaking to Israel, God says,

> Leviticus 26:14-16 ESV
>
> [14] "But if you will not listen to me and will not do all these commandments, [15] if you spurn my statutes and if your soul abhors my rules, so that you will not do all my commandments, but break my covenant, [16] then I will do this to you: ..."

If you continue reading, he promises famine in Verses 19-20. He promises wild beasts will come upon them in Verse 22. In Verse 25, he promises to bring a sword against them, and in the second part of the same verse, he says he will bring pestilence against them if they hide in their walled cities from the sword.

Ezekiel 14:12-23 describes something very similar, with verse 21 saying:

> Ezekiel 14:21 ESV
>
> [21] "For thus says the Lord GOD: How much more when I send upon Jerusalem my four disastrous acts of judgment, sword, famine, wild beasts, and pestilence, to cut off from it man and beast!

God does command sword, pestilence, famine, and wild beast against those who oppose him. When we see it in the Old Testament, we can begin to accept that the rider on the white horse is Christ coming forth to conquer the earth. The tools he used to punish his own people when they worshiped other gods are not reserved for his people alone. God will use them against those who worship the fallen elohim, though God's judgment starts at the house of God.

Still with me? Can we go deeper?

Take a look, if you will, at Habakkuk Chapter 3. Habakkuk was a prophet who lived in the final years before Jerusalem's fall to the Babylonians. In Chapters 1 and 2, he laments what the Assyrians did to the northern kingdom of Israel. It's a back-and-forth between Habakkuk and God. God assures him that the Assyrians will get their due and Babylon will be his weapon against them. Habakkuk, knowing the current state of Judah, realizes that they will be caught up in God's judgment and laments the fact that it is Babylon that will bring it. They are worse than the Assyrians whom God used to judge Northern Israel. Nevertheless, he turns his complaints into a prayer and uses history to praise God for what he will eventually do. Chapter 3 is Habakkuk looking back on what God did in the Exodus to hope for deliverance in the future. I believe what God has done is also what he will do and that is the hope of Habakkuk's prayer.

Verse 2 gives us the subject, *"O Lord..."* and Verse 3 confirms God as the subject, *"God came from Teman* (a city of

Edom) *and from Mount Paran* (a wilderness place west of Edom and south of Canaan, the promised land").

Let's look at Habakkuk 3:5-15, starting with Verse 5.

Habakkuk 3:5 ESV

⁵ Before him (God) went pestilence, and plague followed at his heels. Pest and Plague go with God into Canaan to clear the land for Israel, and pests and plagues are a result of the 4th horseman, whose name is Death and whom Hades follows. Both are sent out by one of the living creatures around God's throne.

⁸ Was your wrath against the rivers, O LORD? Was your anger against the rivers, or your indignation against the sea, when you rode on your horses, on your chariot of salvation?

God is pictured on a horse like the rider on the white horse in Revelation 6:2.

⁹ You stripped the sheath from your bow, calling for many arrows. Here,

God is pictured with a bow like the rider on the white horse in Revelation 6:2.

¹¹ The sun and moon stood still in their place at the light of your arrows as they sped, at the flash of your glittering

spear. ¹² You marched through the earth in fury; you threshed the nations in anger.

Here, God marches through the earth, and in Revelation 6, the four horsemen are called by the four creatures who represent the 4 directions. He also has arrows to go along with the bow of the rider on the white horse. From where does he get his arrows? That's a great question since the rider in Revelation 6 has no arrows.

¹⁴ You pierced with his own arrows the heads of his warriors, who came like a whirlwind to scatter me, rejoicing as if to devour the poor in secret. ¹⁵ You trampled the sea with your horses, the surging of mighty waters.

Here, God is pictured with arrows that he took from the enemy to fill the bow of Verse 9 and again with horses. In Revelation 6:2, the rider on the white horse has a bow, but again no arrows. I'm suggesting he gets them in the same way God did, from his enemies.

Do you see the similarities?

What God did in the Old Testament during the Exodus that Habakkuk is remembering in this praise, the rider on the white horse in Revelation 6, is doing in the New Testament on a global scale. The one on conquest in Revelation 6 is Christ, who is the angel of the Lord in the Old Testament. The one who led God's people out of Egypt. He is on a new mission. Paul says in 1 Corinthians 15:22-26 that *Christ must reign until he has put all his enemies under his feet*, and that is exactly what is being described in Revelation 6. Christ is on conquest, and he is destroying his spiritual enemies and those men who have chosen to serve them.

The Revelation is best explained by the Old Testament. It helps us identify the rider. It is the decoder key. God is depicted in the Old Testament as a rider on a horse carrying a bow and bringing judgments on his enemies, therefore, we can and should easily accept that John has described Christ as the rider on the white horse with a bow in hand and bringing judgment on God's enemies.

Furthermore, I think we must see the riders in the context of the unseen realm. What they carry out in the unseen realm is manifest in the physical world. People feel it, but their first context is the unseen realm, and it is that context I want to focus in on as I conclude this chapter.

I have a few questions for you.

1. What does Habakkuk 3:5 mean when we read pestilence went before God, and plague followed at his heels?
2. In Verse 8, we read a question for God. He's asked, *"Was your wrath against the rivers, your indignation against the*

sea?" What does that mean? Was God mad at the rivers and the sea? What did they do?

3. In Verse 11, we read, *"The sun and moon stood in their place."* They stood at attention in the presence of God. But what should that mean to us? What is the takeaway?

To answer, let me throw some Hebrew words at you:

דֶּבֶר (*dĕ·ḇĕr*) – Pestilence

רֶשֶׁף (*rĕ·šĕp̄*) – Plague

נָהָר (*nā·hār*) – River

יָם (*yām*) – Sea

שֶׁמֶשׁ (*šĕ·mĕš*) – Sun

יָרֵחַ (*yā·rē ͤḥ*) – Moon

These words have one thing in common that is hidden in their English translations. They are names of ancient gods that were worshiped in biblical times. They are all part of the host of heaven. They are members of the unseen realm. Elohim.

Understanding the Bible in its original context is vitally important if we hope to understand it at all. When the original audience read Habakkuk 3, they don't wonder why God is mad at the sea. They know God is angry with the rebellious gods of Deuteronomy 32 and Psalm 82. They don't wonder what it means to have pestilence groveling at Yahweh's feet.

They understand that God demands respect and gets it. Because Peter, James, and John, and the other disciples understand their Bibles, they recognize what is happening when the demons say, *"have you come to torment us before it is time"* and they know why the demons shut up when Jesus tells them to do so. He is the Angel of The Lord, the Son of God, coming to take what is his. He is king, even their king.

The things being described for us in Revelation is the war against the fallen divine creation, and it is muddled and confusing because we try to find the physical world relevance without first identifying its spiritual perspective, or the unseen spiritual context from which it is given. This is especially true when we use our modern world context. Understanding the unseen realm brings a better and fuller understanding of The Revelation. And to the Bible as a whole.

Are you still with me?

Death and Hades

Let's go back to Revelation 6 and look at the fourth horse and its rider, Death with Hades, who follows after him.

We are modern people, so when we read Death and Hades, we see a thing and a place. Death is that unpleasant thing we will all experience and Hades is the place we call Hell where the unsaved go.

Both meanings are correct but is that what the biblical authors are presenting to us?

> Isaiah 28:14-15 ESV
>
> ¹⁴ Therefore hear the word of the LORD, you scoffers, who rule this people in Jerusalem!
>
> ¹⁵ Because you have said, "We have made a covenant with death, and with Sheol, we have an agreement, when the overwhelming whip passes through it will not come to us, for we have made lies our refuge, and in falsehood, we have taken shelter"...

Do you make a covenant with an event and a place? I guess you can, but it makes more sense if what is being presented is a covenant with a foreign god. The people of Israel made a covenant with Death and Sheol. I want to suggest to you that it is the same Death and Hades of Revelation 6, the rider on the fourth horse Death, followed by his cleanup crew, Hades. Their Greek names are Thanatos and Hades. They are the team of Death and Hades.

The point I am trying to make is that the first-century churches who first read The Revelation didn't see an event and a place, they saw Christ commanding his enemies, Death, and Hades. He is turning them on themselves like he did in the Exodus described in Habakkuk 3.

Every time I have referred to the keys belonging to Death and Hell from Revelation 1:18, I referred to them as the keys that once belonged to Death and Hades. John isn't telling us about an event and a place. Instead, he is describing the enemies of God: Death and Hades.

Revelation 6 describes them as riding a horse with the other following, and Revelation 20:13-14 tells us they are thrown into the lake of fire with Satan, which describes exactly what Paul says in 1 Corinthians 15:26. *"The last enemy to be destroyed is Death."*

The personification of Death isn't just here in The Revelation or in one verse in 1 Corinthians 15, it's in Romans 5 as well. Romans 5 is one of the most well-known passages in the Bible, so you might recognize it, *"Therefore, just as sin came into the world through one man, and death through sin, and so death spread to all men because all sinned."* Paul goes on to say, *"Death reigns"* and, *"Sin reigned in Death."* Paul personifies Death (Thanatos) just as John does with the fourth horseman and Isaiah does with the one whom Israel made a covenant with in Isaiah 28. There, his Hebrew name was Mot, the god of death.

Why bring up Romans?

Because I want you to see that these aren't ideas that are reserved for the Prophets of Israel and the weird books of the

Bible like The Revelation. These are themes that are throughout the Bible but hidden by the filters of our modern minds.

Paul says, "Death reigned." The word "reigned" means "to be king."

But here is the good news. Paul says in Ephesians 1:19-22...

> [19] And what is the immeasurable greatness of his (God) power toward us who believe, according to the working of his great might [20] that he worked in Christ when he raised him from the dead and seated him at his right hand in the heavenly places, [21] far above all rule and authority and power and dominion, and above every name that is named, not only in this age but also in the one to come. [22] And he put all things under his feet and gave him as head over all things to the church.

Listen, the good news is that Christ is seated at the right hand, far above all rulers or deities. Death reigned, but Paul puts it in the past tense because he knows the resurrection changed that. Death did reign, but God has elevated Jesus to his right hand and has given him the scroll. Jesus now reigns!

These authorities, dominions, and powers that Paul speaks of are the same rebellious powers of Psalm 82, Isaiah

28, and Revelation 6. They no longer have authority. It has been stripped away and given to our Lord, Jesus Christ.

Do you see how it all ties in? You might be familiar with this one.

> Ephesians 6:10-13
>
> [10] Finally, be strong in the Lord and in the strength of his might. [11] Put on the whole armor of God, that you may be able to stand against the schemes of the devil. [12] For we do not wrestle against flesh and blood, but against the rulers, against the authorities, against the cosmic powers over this present darkness, against the spiritual forces of evil in the heavenly places. [13] Therefore take up the whole armor of God, that you may be able to withstand in the evil day, and having done all, to stand firm...

Can I be honest with you?

I struggle writing this stuff. End times stuff, I mean. I truly don't like it. I don't like it because I have watched the church take this stuff and use it to point their finger and say, "One day you're going to get yours." We read The Revelation with one of those evil smiles, knowing that one day God is going to judge the earth and that all those people who oppose our views are finally going to get theirs. When we do that, we completely miss what Paul says. *"We wrestle not against flesh and blood."* We forget that Peter tells us that God's patience isn't for judgment and wrath. Rather, he tells us that his patience is for repentance.

Paul urges in 1 Timothy 2 that prayer and supplication should be made for all people. Even people in high places, for kings, and for presidents. That is pleasing to God who desires all people to be saved and come to the knowledge of the truth.

Listen, if you've settled in on your high horse waiting for the world to burn, get off it. Hit your knees and pray for your neighbors, for the global church, for your leaders, and for Israel. Pray they come to the knowledge of truth so they can escape the wrath of God as it is poured out on the rebellious and fallen spirits.

One last thing, and it's a cliffhanger. (Or, it would be if I hadn't already made it clear in previous chapters.)

Most people look at The Revelation as something yet to happen, but I see something very different. I see something in progress. It has started, and it is ongoing.

We relate the great end times chapters of Matthew 24, Mark 13, and Luke 21 to things we read in The Revelation. That's legitimate, but what isn't legitimate is ignoring that currently in the world, there are wars, rumors of wars, famines, unclean water, plagues, pestilence, and so much more.

The things Jesus described in Matthew 24, Mark 13, and Luke 21, and the things described in The Revelation have been happening since Jesus' ascension, but all we ever do is recognize them as a "beginning of the end." Every war and every major world event, and even every time a president from another party wins an election, we think the tribulation is near. I'm suggesting that these things are part of the conquest described by Paul in 1 Corinthians 15:22-26 and what John describes beginning in Revelation 6. I suggest they are ongoing.

We will talk more about that in the next chapter, but if you can even grasp that as a possibility. If you can even imagine that I might be right, that these things are ongoing, I want to ask you a question.

What is your role? What part are you playing?

In Revelation 6, the rider has a bow but no arrows. I find that odd, but I believe it is because you are the arrows. Remember that in Habakkuk 3, God took arrows from the enemy, but your job isn't to bring death to men. It is to bring life. You're the carriers of the gospel. The rider on the horse is spreading the gospel, the good news that a new king reigns. Like God in Habakkuk 3, who called for many arrows, Jesus is calling for arrows to spread the gospel. Each new believer is notched into his bow and shot into a dark world, taking back the nations, defeating the unseen enemies, winning souls, and spreading light. We are the enemy's arrows turned against him, just like in Habakkuk 3. That's your role. That's our role. The great commission. Make disciples of all men.

God help us do it! Amen.

Has Been Coming Violently

In the previous chapter, I left you with a real cliff hanger. I presented The Revelation as something that has started and is ongoing, and I am sure you would like an explanation. That is what I hope to do at this point, so let's dive in.

The Revelation is not future only. It is present and ongoing. It began at the commencement of the Kingdom, and the kingdom, according to Jesus, has been going forth violently since the time of John the Baptist.

> Matthew 11:12 ESV
>
> ¹² From the days of John the Baptist until now, the kingdom of heaven has suffered violence, and the violent take it by force. Many Bibles, like the ESV, will have a footnote adding, "or, 'has been coming violently.'"

The kingdom started with John the Baptist, but it really cranked up with the words, *"It is finished,"* spoken by Jesus from the cross. Shortly after, the powers of this world realized the mistake they had made.

> 1 Corinthians 2:8 ESV
>
> None of the rulers of this age understood this, for if they had, they would not have crucified the Lord of glory.

From that time forward the powers have been under attack by the reigning king. He is on offense.

> 1 Corinthians 15:22-27 ESV
>
> ²² For as in Adam all die, so also in Christ shall all be made alive. (Resurrection) ²³ But each in his own order: Christ the firstfruits, then at his coming those who belong to Christ. ²⁴ Then comes the end, when he delivers the kingdom to God the Father after destroying every rule and every authority and power. ²⁵ For **he must reign until** he has put all his enemies under his feet. ²⁶ The last enemy to be destroyed is death. ²⁷ For "God **has put all things** in subjection under his feet..."

Jesus reigns! We've determined that. Jesus, having had all things subjected to him, is going out with bow in hand.

> Revelation 6:1-2 ESV
>
> Now, I watched when the Lamb opened one of the seven seals, and I heard one of the four living creatures say with a voice like thunder, "Come!" ² And I looked, and behold, a white horse! And its rider had a bow, and a crown was given to him, and he came out conquering, and to conquer.

In the last chapter, we identified this rider on the white horse as Christ. Christ is the rider with the bow in his hand. He came, as prophesied, to the tents of Judah first. He came to Jerusalem.

> Zechariah 12:7 ESV
>
> "And the LORD will give salvation to the tents of Judah first..."

Jesus came to Jerusalem, the capitol of Judah, and he hung on a cross and brought salvation to the world. However, this salvation first came to Judah just as Zechariah prophesied, and Paul confirms in Romans 1:16 where he says, *"I am not ashamed of the gospel. It is the power of God unto salvation to the Jew first..."* This began, as we said above, when John the Baptist began to preach in the wilderness of Judea, **"Repent, for the kingdom of God is at hand" (Matthew 3:2).** Salvation and the kingdom of God are synonymous.

Here is what I want you to see. The story John is telling us in Revelation, with all its seals, bowls, thunders, and trumpets, began with Jesus. He came conquering and to conquer. He is spreading kingdom.

Look at Zechariah 9.

> Zechariah 9:9-13 ESV
>
> [9] Rejoice greatly, O daughter of Zion! Shout aloud, O daughter of Jerusalem! Behold, your king is coming to

you; righteous and having salvation is he, humble and mounted on a donkey, on a colt, the foal of a donkey.

Sound familiar? This is the prophecy fulfilled by Jesus as he rode into Jerusalem, on a young donkey. It foretells of the triumphal entry just before Jesus is crucified.

> [10] I will cut off the chariot from Ephraim and the war horse from Jerusalem; and the battle bow shall be cut off, and he shall speak peace to the nations; his rule shall be from sea to sea, and from the River to the ends of the earth.
>
> [11] As for you also, because of the blood of my covenant with you, I will set your prisoners free from the waterless pit.
>
> [12] Return to your stronghold, O prisoners of hope; today, I declare that I will restore to you double.
>
> [13] For I have bent Judah as my bow; I have made Ephraim its arrow. I will stir up your sons, O Zion, against your sons, O Greece, and wield you like a warrior's sword.

This is a messianic prophecy. It told the Jews a savior was coming to deliver them. He comes humble but he is armed, and he has as his weapon the bow of Judah Ephraim as his arrows.

The bow of Judah lines up nicely with Revelation 6:1-2. The rider on the white horse has a bow, and that rider is the one who came to Jerusalem humble and riding on a donkey. He is Jesus. His bow is Judah, the Jews. You will likely know the apostles are all Jews. You will know Jesus' disciples, including the 70, are Jews. You will probably know that those in the upper room, the 120, are Jews. And you will likely know that on the day of Pentecost, Jerusalem was filled with Jews from all over the known world. It was those Jews who heard the message and took the gospel to the nations. They are the first to hear, and they are the bent bow.

But what of the arrows? In the previous chapter, I told you, "*you are the arrows*" but here we are told the arrows are Ephraim. Ephraim is one of Joseph's two sons. The other Manasseh. We will see one of the two in just a bit when we get into chapter 7 and the sealed 144,000 Jews. That will be Manasseh, but what of Ephraim?

Right before Jacob died, he gathered his 12 sons to bless them (Genesis 49). Before that Joseph bought his two sons Manasseh and Ephraim to be blessed. Manasseh being the oldest should have received the right hand of blessing, but something happened.

Genesis 48:14-19 ESV

¹⁴ And Israel stretched out his right hand and laid it on the head of Ephraim, who was the younger, and his left hand on the head of Manasseh, crossing his hands (for Manasseh was the firstborn).

¹⁵ And he blessed Joseph and said, "The God before whom my fathers Abraham and Isaac walked, the God who has been my shepherd all my life long to this day,

¹⁶ the angel who has redeemed me from all evil, bless the boys; and in them let my name be carried on, and the name of my fathers Abraham and Isaac; and let them grow into a multitude in the midst of the earth."

¹⁷ When Joseph saw that his father laid his right hand on the head of Ephraim, it displeased him, and he took his father's hand to move it from Ephraim's head to Manasseh's head. ¹⁸ And Joseph said to his father, "Not this way, my father; since this one is the firstborn, put your right hand on his head." ¹⁹ But his father refused and said, "I know, my son, I know. He also shall become a people, and he also shall be great. Nevertheless, his younger brother shall be greater than he, and his offspring shall become a multitude of nations."

Did you catch that? Ephraim's offspring will be a multitude of nations.

Judah is the bow in the hand of the conqueror of Revelation 6, Jesus, the rider on the white horse. The arrows, the ammunition for the bow, is Ephraim who is a multitude of nations.

Paul said in Romans 1:16, *"For I am not ashamed of the gospel, for it is the power of God for salvation to everyone who believes, to the Jew first and also to the Greek."* Everywhere he went, Paul lived by this principle, going first to share the gospel in the synagogues among the Jews. But in Acts 13, we see his frustration.

> Acts 13:44-49 ESV
>
> ⁴⁴ The next Sabbath almost the whole city gathered to hear the word of the Lord. ⁴⁵ But when the Jews saw the crowds, they were filled with jealousy and began to contradict what was spoken by Paul, reviling him. ⁴⁶ And Paul and Barnabas spoke out boldly, saying, **"It was necessary that the word of God be spoken first to you.** Since you thrust it aside and judge yourselves unworthy of eternal life, behold, we are turning to the Gentiles. ⁴⁷ For so the Lord has commanded us, saying,

> "'I have made you a light for the Gentiles, that you may bring salvation to the ends of the earth.'"

⁴⁸ And when the Gentiles heard this, they began rejoicing and glorifying the word of the Lord, and as many as were appointed to eternal life believed. ⁴⁹ And the word of the Lord was spreading throughout the whole region.

The Greek word (ethnos) for Gentiles is the word for nations. It can be translated as "Gentiles" or "nations." With the bow of Judah bent, Paul puts the arrow of the multitude of nations in the bow. That multitude is known as Ephraim, aka the Gentiles or nations, and spreads the gospel with them.

Christ, the rider on the white horse, with bow in hand, has begun his conquest. He has come to reclaim what is his. He is making war on the unseen enemies, and we, with our Jewish brothers, are his weapons. They are the bow; we are the arrows. Do you remember Habakkuk 3 where God used the arrows of his enemies against them? We are the enemy's arrows taken from our former master and used against him. The kingdom is going forward by the hand of those delivered from the now-defeated king.

With that in mind and having previously looked at the events of Chapter 6 and their supernatural context, let's look at Chapter 7.

Verses 1-8 tell us 12,000 Jews from each of the 12 tribes of Israel are sealed. This identifies a remnant, a sufficient remnant, which. means that Jewish heritage alone is not enough to be sealed. Some, but not all, are sealed.

Remember our rules:

1. The Unseen Realm is real, and it matters in understanding what John is communicating.
2. John uses the Old Testament, and what he uses and how he uses it matters to the understanding of the vision.

First, the sealing is in the unseen realm and does not appear as an actual mark on their heads or anywhere else. It marks them safe from the judgment that is coming and is meant to be a sign to unseen forces that are bringing God's judgment. The seal is not for other people to see.

Second, we find an Old Testament anchor in Ezekiel 9. As God prepares to judge Jerusalem with the armies of Babylon, he sends an angel through the city to mark those he describes as sighing and groaning over the things that are happening in Jerusalem. After they are marked, he sends destroying angels through the city to judge all those who are not marked. The mark is not seen in the physical realm; it is for the unseen destroying angels made by an unseen angel scribe.

God preserves a remnant. He marks off some, but not all. He will not destroy all of Israel. They are his beloved. Speaking of Israel, the prophet Isaiah says...

> Isaiah 27:7-8 ESV
>
> [7] Has he struck them as he struck those who struck them? Or have they been slain as their slayers were slain?
>
> [8] Measure by measure, by exile, you contended with them; he removed them with his fierce breath in the day of the east wind.

He does not deal with Israel with complete destruction. Rather, through exile, he judges them, and he keeps a remnant.

Paul recognizes as much and reminds his readers that God always preserves a remnant.

> Romans 11:1-5 ESV
>
> I ask, then, has God rejected his people? By no means! For I myself am an Israelite, a descendant of Abraham, a member of the tribe of Benjamin. [2] God has not rejected his people whom he foreknew. Do you not

know what the Scripture says of Elijah, and how he appeals to God against Israel? [3] "Lord, they have killed your prophets, they have demolished your altars, and I alone am left, and they seek my life." [4] But what is God's reply to him? "I have kept for myself seven thousand men who have not bowed the knee to Baal." [5] So too, at the present time, there is a remnant, chosen by grace.

I want you to focus on that last line, "*So too at the present time there is a remnant chosen by grace.*" This is like the remnant of Revelation 7. God has preserved a remnant of his beloved Israel. He always has. He always will. I believe Paul and John are talking about the same group of people. This is a continued remnant. God began preserving Jewish believers in the first century and still does today.

The list of tribes in Chapter 7 includes Manasseh, who replaces Dan but not Ephraim. Instead, we see Joseph, their father. Why is that? Why is it not both Manasseh and Ephraim?

Joseph is put in Ephraim's spot to preserve the whole of Israel, the 12 tribes, while Ephraim is represented in the following passage. Remember, Ephraim is a multitude of nations (Genesis 48:19). In Revelation 7, beginning in Verse 9 just after the remnant of Israel we read:

Revelation 7:9-10 ESV

⁹ After this, I looked, and behold, a great multitude that no one could number, from every nation, from all tribes and peoples and languages, standing before the throne and before the Lamb, clothed in white robes, with palm branches in their hands, ¹⁰ and crying out with a loud voice, "Salvation belongs to our God who sits on the throne, and to the Lamb!"

The 144,000 represent the bow, while the multitude represent the arrows. They are Ephraim, a multitude of nations. They are people from all nations, tribes, peoples, and languages.

Time is a problem here, so I will need to leave it there for now saying only this: This multitude are all those that die in Christ since his death and resurrection. The multitude John sees is currently present in heaven and growing with the death of every believer. I am suggesting that the death of every believer since Christ was enthroned in Heaven is an injustice at the hands of enemy combatants, the unseen enemies. Those dead stand in Heaven as witnesses against God's enemies, and his enemies will pay.

I believe these are the same souls that John sees under the altar in Revelation 6

Revelation 6:9-11 ESV

> ⁹ When he opened the fifth seal, I saw under the altar the souls of those who had been slain for the word of God and for the witness they had borne. ¹⁰ They cried out with a loud voice, "O Sovereign Lord, holy and true, how long before you will judge and avenge our blood on those who dwell on the earth?" ¹¹ Then they were each given a white robe and told to rest a little longer until the number of their fellow servants and their brothers should be complete, who were to be killed as they themselves had been.

Their prayers and cries for justice are what fill the bowl of incense in the first few verses of Chapter 8.

Revelation 8:3-5 ESV

> ³ And another angel came and stood at the altar with a golden censer, and he was given much incense to offer with the prayers of all the saints on the golden altar before the throne, ⁴ and the smoke of the incense, with the prayers of the saints, rose before God from the hand of the angel. ⁵ Then the angel took the censer and filled it with fire from the altar and threw it on the earth, and there were peals of thunder, rumblings, flashes of lightning, and an earthquake.

These prayers are what brings on the seven trumpet judgments. In Chapter 8, we see several things happen as the result of seven angels blowing seven trumpets.

The first is hail, fire, and blood. The blood shouldn't be seen as blood falling from heaven, but it is the reason the judgments have come. It is the blood of the saints from Chapters 6 and 7 that prompt the 7seven trumpets. Their unjust deaths have brought judgment on the world.

The first trumpet brings wild weather patterns. The second and third trumpets are a star and a great mountain that fall from the sky, while the fourth brings about darkness with a third of the lights in the sky going dark, (the sun, moon, and stars). While some insist these should be interpreted literally, we have already placed this in their correct context. These are not stars and mountains. They are not comets or asteroids. A third of the stars do not go dark. These are members of the unseen realm used as tools of judgment on the fallen members of the unseen realm. People of the ancient world didn't know what a star was and certainly didn't realize how far they were from the earth. When they looked at the sky, they saw the heavenly host, deities. They saw the gods. They saw the host of heaven.

When John describes stars falling to earth, he sees angels. Remember:

Revelation 9:1 ESV

> And the fifth angel blew his trumpet, and I saw a star fallen from heaven to earth, and he was given the key to the shaft of the bottomless pit.

Do comets get keys to open locked pits? No. When John sees a great mountain, he sees a member of the unseen realm.

Psalm 68:15-16 ESV

> [15] O mountain of God (the gods), mountain of Bashan; O many-peaked mountain, mountain of Bashan!
>
> [16] Why do you look with hatred, O many-peaked mountain, at the mount that God desired for his abode, yes, where the LORD will dwell forever?

Do mountains envy or hate? No. Bashan is home to the fallen elohim. It isn't the mountain that hates. It is its inhabitants that hate the mountain of God. (Bashan is home to Mount Hermon, the place where the book of Enoch describes the rebellion of the angels took place.)

When John sees a third of the heavenly lights go out, he doesn't see a mass eclipse, he sees members of the unseen realm fall from their posts.

Revelation 12:4 ESV

> ³ And another sign appeared in heaven: behold, a great red dragon, with seven heads and ten horns, and on his heads seven diadems. ⁴ His tail swept down a third of the stars of heaven and cast them to the earth.

You probably recognize this verse because it is the verse used to teach that a third of the angels followed Satan. I've mentioned it before. Stars are angels. The point is, these aren't natural disasters, nor are they weapons of modern warfare, they are what happens in the spiritual world while God is judging the fallen members of divine creation. The Old Testament is full of it. I've referred to it previously. Habakkuk 3, Isaiah 24:21-23, Isaiah 13, Isaiah 34, Psalm 22, Psalm 68 and Psalm 82. There's more, but I don't have space to add them here.

We should be confident, however, that these things have consequences in our world. Even now we see these things playing out. There are wars, famines, plagues, and pestilence. Wildfires rage, the earth rumbles with earthquakes, and there are terrible storms and tsunamis. Parts of the world are barren and covered with sand, and other parts have water, but it isn't clean and will make you sick. I think it is a terrible mistake to look, from the comfort of our homes here in America, for the world to get a lot worse when there are parts of the world where the end seems to have come already. It would be hard to convince people in some parts of the world that it could get much worse.

Let's look quickly at Chapter 9. I want to look at this because, in an earlier chapter, we talked about the armies of God that came to deliver Elisha from the Syrian army.

Earlier we mentioned Revelation 9:1 and were introduced to a star that is given the keys to the bottomless pit. There is debate about this angel, but I believe this is a good angel in that he is not a member of the rebellious host, and he is on a mission from God. He has been commissioned to release the army of fallen heavenly beings so that they can be judged.

They are presented as follows:

> Revelation 9:3 ESV
>
> [3] Then from the smoke came locusts on the earth, and they were given power like the power of scorpions of the earth.

These are not real locusts. They are told not to harm the grass, green plants, or trees but only those people who do not have the seal of God. That's the opposite of what locusts do. I believe this to be the angels that Jude and Peter tell us about.

> Jude 6 ESV
>
> [6] And the angels who did not stay within their own position of authority, but left their proper dwelling, he

has kept in eternal chains under gloomy darkness until the judgment of the great day:

2 Peter 2:4 ESV

⁴ For if God did not spare angels when they sinned, but cast them into hell and committed them to chains of gloomy darkness to be kept until the judgment...

(See also Isaiah 24:21-23)

The fallen angels kept in chains are what John describes as locusts. They are what is released from the pit.

Let's look at a bit more.

Revelation 9:7-11 ESV

⁷ In appearance, the locusts were like horses prepared for battle: on their heads were what looked like crowns of gold; their faces were like human faces, ⁸ their hair like women's hair, and their teeth like lions' teeth; ⁹ they had breastplates like breastplates of iron, and the noise of their wings was like the noise of many chariots with horses rushing into battle. ¹⁰ They have tails and stings like scorpions, and their power to hurt people for five months is in their tails. ¹¹ They have as king over them the angel of the bottomless pit. His name in Hebrew is Abaddon, and in Greek, he is called Apollyon.

The identity of their leader is a subject of debate, but I believe it is Satan. He is released from the bottomless pit himself in Revelation 20:7-8, but that discussion will have to wait for now. In Revelation 9:6, we are told the people long to die, but death will flee from them, but under the judgment of the sixth trumpet, death comes to a third. We will consider who that is at a late point.

I stated earlier that what happens in the unseen realm has real-world consequences. So, what is described in Revelation 9:13-19 is likely an earthly military force gathered to make war because of the unseen forces let loose from the bottomless pit. A couple of passages found later in the Revelation explain exactly that.

Revelation 16:12-15

^{12} The sixth angel poured out his bowl on the great river Euphrates, and its water was dried up, to prepare the way for the kings from the east. ^{13} And I saw, coming out of the mouth of the dragon and out of the mouth of the beast and out of the mouth of the false prophet, three unclean spirits like frogs. ^{14} For they are demonic spirits, performing signs, who go abroad to the kings of the whole world, to assemble them for battle on the great day of God the Almighty. ^{15} (**"Behold, I am coming like a thief! Blessed is the one who stays awake, keeping his garments on, that he may not**

go about naked and be seen exposed!") ‍¹⁶ And they assembled them at the place that in Hebrew is called Armageddon.

This passage may beg the question, "How can a passage from chapter 16 explain what happens in Chapter 9?" That will have to wait until later as well.

Chapter 10 is Jesus appearing to John with a scroll in hand. He pronounces seven thunder judgments, but they are kept from us. He has a scroll in his hand. It is likely the scroll from chapter 5. John is told to take the scroll and eat it. It will be sweet to the taste, but bitter in his stomach. This is like Ezekiel 2 and 3 where Ezekiel is told to eat a scroll. In Ezekiel, the scroll has words of lamentation, mourning, and woe. Very simply, this reminds those of us who belong to the Lord, who will escape final judgment and who may find God's judgment pleasing at first, that judgment is bitter. People we love and care about will be caught up in it.

Now let's close this chapter by considering Revelation 11 and the two witnesses. I think we will find that it fits nicely with what has just gone before. The world is being judged, but God's people seem to escape the judgment. They've been sealed. It is like the Exodus account and the blood that kept Death from plaguing their homes. While the world suffers like Egypt, Israel is doing okay. The deception used to bring the world's armies to their doorstep may be that it is they who have caused it all and, therefore, must pay. The beast that rises from the bottomless pit and gathers the armies of the world brings them to the Holy City to make the Jews pay. (Revelation 11:7-8)

The Two Witnesses

> Revelation 11:3-4 ESV
>
> ³ And I will grant authority to my two witnesses, and they will prophesy for 1,260 days, clothed in sackcloth."
>
> ⁴ These are the two olive trees and the two lampstands that stand before the Lord of the earth.

Who are the Two Witnesses?

Traditional Views hold the following interpretations of the two witnesses:

First, Moses and Elijah: The miracles performed by the two witnesses are similar to those of Moses and Elijah and It is Moses and Elijah that appear in the transfiguration.

Next, Elijah and Enoch: Neither man died, they were both taken into heaven. Therefore, many commentators, using, "*it is appointed unto man once to die*" suppose that Elijah and Enoch are sent back to die their appointed time.

Alternate View

The two witnesses are representative of something else and not individuals. The two witnesses are representative of Judah and Israel, the Southern and Northern kingdoms returned from exile. This is the view that I hold. We can know they are representative of groups and not individuals because of Verse 4.

> Revelation 11:4 ESV
>
> [4] These are the two olive trees and the two lampstands that stand before the Lord of the earth.

In Revelation 1, lampstands represent churches, bodies of believers, not individuals.

> Revelation 1:20 ESV
>
> [20] As for the mystery of the seven stars that you saw in my right hand and the seven golden lampstands, the seven stars are the angels of the seven churches, and the seven lampstands are the seven churches.

Of help here will be our second rule to understanding The Revelation. John uses the Old Testament, and what he uses, and how he uses it matters if we want to understand the vision.

Here, John is referring to Zechariah 4:1-3.

Zechariah 4:1-3 ESV

¹ And the angel who talked with me came again and woke me, like a man who is awakened out of his sleep. ² And he said to me, "What do you see?" I said, "I see, and behold, a lampstand all of gold, with a bowl on the top of it, and seven lamps on it, with seven lips on each of the lamps that are on the top of it. ³ And there are two olive trees by it, one on the right of the bowl and the other on its left."

Right away, we see the reference. There are two olive trees, the same as what John sees in Revelation 11, but there is one problem. John is told the two witnesses are the two olive trees and two lampstands that stand before the Lord. In Zechariah 4, we only have one.

Why?

We need to consider the historical context. Zechariah was writing in the postexilic period and only the Southern Kingdom had returned, thus one lampstand. The Northern Kingdom was still in exile; thus, its lamp isn't present before the Lord. He had removed their lampstand.

Is that possible? Does God remove lampstands? He does. In Revelation 2, writing to the church in Ephesus, we read...

Revelation 2:4-5 ESV

⁴ But I have this against you, that you have abandoned the love you had at first. ⁵ Remember therefore from where you have fallen; repent, and do the works you did at first. If not, I will come to you and remove your lampstand from its place, unless you repent.

The Northern Kingdom had not repented of their idolatry and had not returned. Their lampstand was removed, but we know they will come back.

Ezekiel 37:15-21 ESV

¹⁵ The word of the LORD came to me: ¹⁶ "Son of man, take a stick and write on it, 'For Judah, and the people of Israel associated with him'; then take another stick and write on it, 'For Joseph (the stick of Ephraim) and all the house of Israel associated with him.' ¹⁷ And join them one to another into one stick, that they may become one in your hand. ¹⁸ And when your people say to you, 'Will you not tell us what you mean by these?' ¹⁹ say to them, Thus says the Lord GOD: Behold, I am about to take the stick of Joseph **(that is in the hand of Ephraim)** and the tribes of Israel associated with him. And I will join with it the stick of Judah, and make them one stick, that they may be one in my hand. ²⁰ When the sticks on which you write are in your hand before their eyes, ²¹ then say to them, Thus says the

Lord GOD: Behold, I will take the people of Israel from the nations among which they have gone, and will gather them from all around, and bring them to their own land.

The Hebrew word for stick is עץ (ʿēṣ) and is defined as a tree, i.e., as any kind of relatively large woody plant. (DBL) It is like a branch from an olive tree.

The two witnesses stand for Israel. They represent both houses of Israel, Judah, and Israel. John says the following about them:

Revelation 11:6 ESV

They have the power to shut the sky, that no rain may fall during the days of their prophesying, and they have power over the waters to turn them into blood and to strike the earth with every kind of plague,, as often as they desire.

And we are told:

Revelation 11:7 ESV

[7] And when they have finished their testimony, the beast that rises from the bottomless pit will make war on them and conquer them and kill them...

I believe because the world blames them for everything that is happening, the beast that rises from the bottomless pit, (i.e., the dragon from Revelation 20:7-8 along with the beast and the false prophet from Revelation 16:13-1) deceive the nations to come against Israel. This, I believe, is what is being described in Revelation 9.

The armies gathered against Israel appear to have won. For three and a half days, Israel seems defeated. The enemy has won, so his earthly followers believe, but much like when Jesus' body was in the tomb, they were wrong. Something happens, and they are resurrected and called into Heaven.

Revelation 11:8-12 ESV

...and their dead bodies will lie in the streets of the great city that symbolically is called Sodom and Egypt, where their Lord was crucified. [9] For three and a half days, some from the peoples and tribes and languages and nations will gaze at their dead bodies and refuse to let them be placed in a tomb, [10] and those who dwell on the earth will rejoice over them and make merry and exchange presents, because these two prophets had been a torment to those who dwell on the earth. [11] But after the three and a half days, a breath of life from God entered them, and they stood up on their feet, and great fear fell on those who saw them. [12] Then they heard a loud voice from heaven saying to them, "Come up here!" And they went up to heaven in a cloud, and their enemies watched them.

Chapter 11 closes with the final trumpet, the seventh trumpet blast. I believe this is the trumpet blast described in 1 Corinthians 15:51-53.

1 Corinthians 15:51-53 ESV

[51] Behold! I tell you a mystery. We shall not all sleep, but we shall all be changed, [52] in a moment, in the twinkling of an eye, at the last trumpet. For the trumpet will sound, and the dead will be raised imperishable, and we shall be changed. [53] For this perishable body must put on the imperishable, and this mortal body must put on immortality.

This is the last thing to happen before the Lord returns and his throne is set in Jerusalem.

Don't you want to be a part of it? I mean a part of the whole thing. I want to be a part of both the coming of the kingdom and experience the arrival of the king. I want to be among those who are bringing the kingdom of God by defeating the fallen Elohim, taking from them more arrows to be used against them.

Completing The Rule Book

Over the last five chapters we've only just begun to scratch the surface of The Revelation. In this chapter, I hope to give you a few more rules that will help you continue your own study as we begin to wind down. These will build on the previous two rules we've used throughout the book.

Our rules so far are these:

1. The Unseen Realm is real, and it matters to John.

John has been invited into Heaven and thus relates to us events from a heavenly (spiritual) perspective. We've added to that, the idea his language reflects the culture of his day, not ours. Stars aren't stars, for example, they are the host of heaven, spiritual beings.

2. John uses the Old Testament, and what he uses and how he uses it matters if we are to understand the vision.

John is very familiar with scripture, and he uses it to express what he sees in the vision. Hopefully, this rule is encouraging you to become more familiar with your Bibles. A growing knowledge of the Old Testament will help us better understand John and the other New Testament authors.

Very simply, we should understand that much of what John sees is taking place behind a veil in the spiritual world, and he is using the Old Testament to help us understand it.

Stars and mountains falling from the sky and dragons that pull a third of the stars to the ground are not physical realities, but windows into the spiritual battle that rages between God and his armies and Satan and his armies. See Revelation 12.

I am not denying that there are and will be physical realities as a result of these spiritual battles. There will be. When spirits battle, things happen in our world. When the angels fought against the Prince of Persia in Daniel 10, the Prince of Persia was deposed, and the Prince of Greece took his place. In history, we see that Greece conquered Persia and replaced it as the dominant world power.

Again, our rules are:

1. The Unseen Realm is real, and it matters to us like it mattered to John.
2. John uses the Old Testament to describe what he sees, and a better understanding of the Old Testament will help us understand the Revelation.

Not All of The Revelation is Future

Our next rule is to understand that not all of the Revelation is future.

John opens with, *"The revelation of Jesus Christ, which God gave him to show to his servants the things that must soon take place."* Revelation 1:1

In Verse 3, he says, *"Blessed is the one who reads aloud the words of this prophecy, and blessed are those who hear, and who keep what is written in it, for the time is near."*

There's a big debate that rages about when John wrote The Revelation. Some say he did so in the late 60's AD before the destruction of the Temple in 70 AD. Others say mid 90's AD. Either way, it is some 2000 years ago. Surely, this isn't what John means by soon. John doesn't define *"soon"* as roughly 2000 years. And surely, he doesn't describe two millennia and counting as being *"near"* in time.

John goes on to say that he is the reader's *"brother in tribulation and the kingdom, and the patient endurance"*. John's description gives me the feeling that John is describing something that has started and may last a long time. The persecution that is described in Revelation was ongoing in John's time. He didn't choose the lovely isle of Patmos as a place to gain inspiration for his book. He was exiled there by the Romans because of the word of God. He was being persecuted and imprisoned. His fellow apostles were being murdered, and even his own disciples. One of which John mentions in Revelation 2:13. His name was Antipas.

It is very easy for us to sit on our leather couches and, during commercial breaks, talk about the pain that is coming during the tribulation while ignoring the pain the early church felt and people all over the world feel today: famine, plague and pestilence, wars and rumors of wars, persecution. It happens today and on grand scales that we in America are mostly immune from. These aren't future events. These things happened in the past and are present and ongoing.

Revelation 4 and 5 paint a great courtroom scene. God is on his throne when his star witness walks in, the spotless lamb. When did this happen?

John is seeing what Daniel before him saw in Daniel 7:13. The son of man coming on the clouds and standing before the ancient of Days who is seated on his throne and passing judgment. Jesus told the high priest in Matthew 26:64 that he was that son of man, coming on the clouds and that he would soon know it. His resurrection was the sign that he had told the truth. In Acts 1:9, we see Jesus leave his disciples and ascend into the heavens on a cloud, and I believe he was ushered directly into the throne room of God. When he enters, he is the son of man Daniel describes in Daniel 7 and he is the lamb that John describes in Revelation 5. Daniel sees the future, and John sees what was recent history to him, something that had taken place in his lifetime. Jesus has taken his place on the throne at the right hand of the Father. He reigns.

Check that off the list because it is done.

Revelation 12:1-5 describes the birth of a child who will rule with a rod of iron. That's a messianic promise from Psalm 2:9, and it was fulfilled with the birth of Jesus in the first century. Do we agree?

Check it off the list. It is done.

The child born is caught up to God and to his throne in Verse 5. That happened at the ascension, as I described above. Do we agree?

Again, check it off the list. It is done.

When engaging with Revelation be open to the idea that not all of it happens in the future. Some of it has taken place, and much of it is ongoing. Jesus is reigning and will reign until all his enemies are put under his feet. The last one will be Death.

Understanding the Intermissions.

Our next rule to follow when engaging the Revelation is understanding the Intermissions.

An intermission is a recess between parts of a performance or production. In The Revelation, there are several intermissions. John wants us to get up and stretch, get some popcorn, and maybe some caffeine. He wants us fresh for what comes next. We need to be open to the idea that The Revelation is not a linear chronology. It isn't a straight timeline meant to be read from earlier to later events. I mentioned this in a previous chapter when I suggested Revelation 16 explains Revelation 9 and 11.

Here's another example. Chapter 12 does not follow Chapter 11 on a timeline.

Leading up to Chapter 11, we see the lamb having already been slain and standing before the throne of God in Revelation 5. Most of the seven seals and seven trumpets blow in Chapters 6 through 9. The armies of Hell are released in Chapter 9. The two witnesses are killed in Chapter 11, as we talked about in the last chapter, and the last trumpet blows as 11 closes. Then, in Chapter 12, Christ is born. At least, that is how you will need to read it if you take Revelation to be a linear chronology where events happen on a strict timeline.

Chapter 17 does not follow Chapter 16 on a timeline.

Chapter 16 ends with the armies of the world coming against Jerusalem and being destroyed. In Verse 17, the seventh and final bowl of judgment is poured out, and a voice from heaven shouts, "It is done!" Well, it is done except for the judgment of the woman who sits upon the beast, who was just destroyed but will be destroyed again in Chapter 18. This is, of course, if you read The Revelation as a timeline where things happen one thing after the next.

We should read the Revelation as having acts like in a play. There are breaks, or intermissions, in which we can pause, regroup, and then begin again. These Acts, when they are put together, tell the whole story. Each act progresses the audience little by little to the end of the story. Each filling in details, adding and removing characters, but each coming to the same conclusion.

Here is how I divide the book:

- Chapters 1-3 are an introduction, like any good letter.
- Chapters 4-11 are the first telling of the story, which begins at Christ's ascension and arrival in the throne room after his obedience to the cross and progresses to the final battle in Jerusalem. It includes the death and resurrection of the two witnesses and the opening of the heavenly temple.
- Chapters 12-16 are the retelling of the story, beginning with Christ's birth and ending with the final battle in Jerusalem, followed by a voice in heaven saying, "It is done." This version introduces us to Satan, the Beast, and the false prophet.
- Chapters 17-19 fill in the details of the beast and Babylon and Jesus' ultimate triumph over them, ending with the final battle. (Repeated from Chapter 11, 14:17-20 and Chapter 16)

- Chapter 20 briefly retells the story with an emphasis on Jesus' defeat of Satan, Death, and Hades, including the nations from the four corners. Death is the final enemy to be destroyed, Revelation 20:14.
- Chapters 21-22 are the finale. Eden returns to earth. The new Jerusalem.

Here's how this works. The closing of Chapters 21-22 could be at the end of Chapter 11, 16, 19, or right where it is after Chapter 20. Each section is retelling the same story with different perspectives and or with an emphasis on different characters, but they all end the same way.

Recapitulation

If John is retelling the story over and over, you are bound to see some of the same events, and you do. It is called recapitulation. **Recapitulation is defined as an act of summarizing and restating the main points of something. John recaps key points.** Let's look at a few of the things John recapitulates (recaps) throughout the book.

In Chapter 11, the beast who came from the bottomless pit (Chapter 9) makes war on the two witnesses who we learned, represent Israel.

Revelation 9:1

> And the fifth angel blew his trumpet, and I saw a star fallen from heaven to earth, and he was given the key to the shaft of the bottomless pit.

From the bottomless pit comes an army of locusts.

Revelation 9:11

> They have as king over them the angel of the bottomless pit. His name in Hebrew is Abaddon, and in Greek, he is called Apollyon.

The names mean destruction and destroyer.

And in Revelation 11:7-8 we read:

> And when they have finished their testimony, the beast that rises from the bottomless pit will make war on them and conquer them and kill them, ⁸ and their dead bodies will lie in the street of the great city that symbolically is called Sodom and Egypt, where their Lord was crucified.

Verse 9 says, *"For three and a half days some from the peoples and tribes and languages and nations will gaze at their dead bodies..."* and in Revelation 11:18, we see the 24 elders worshiping God for destroying the destroyers of the earth.

Then, in Revelation 16:13-14 we read:

And I saw, coming out of the mouth of the dragon and out of the mouth of the beast and out of the mouth of the false prophet, three unclean spirits like frogs. [14] For they are demonic spirits, performing signs, who go abroad to the kings of the whole world, to assemble them for battle on the great day of God the Almighty.

In Verse 15, we read that they gathered in a place called Armageddon. There is good evidence that Armageddon should be translated as the Mountain of God, aka Jerusalem, but I don't have the space to do that here.

In 19:19, the armies of the earth, with the beast, gather to make war against the rider on the white horse.

Revelation 19:19

[19] And I saw the beast and the kings of the earth with their armies gathered to make war against him who was sitting on the horse and against his army.

And in Revelation 20:7-10 we read:

[7] And when the thousand years are ended, Satan will be released from his prison [8] and will come out to deceive the nations that are at the four corners of the earth, Gog and Magog, to gather them for battle; their number is like the sand of the sea.

There's an obvious question we need to answer: Are these different battles, or are they the same battle retold as part of each act or section?

Should we read Chapters 4-11 and then pause before reading 12-16, and then pause again before consuming 17-19, and then pause one more time before reading the last act where God deals with the major players, Satan, Death, and Hades, Chapter 20? Yes. The answer is yes.

I believe each of the above sections describes the same gathering of God's enemies as John recapitulates the story, providing new perspectives. Each of these battles describe the Gog/Magog war.

Let's recap, pun intended, before we add any further rules.

So far, our rules to understand The Revelation include:

- Knowing the Unseen Realm is real, and it matters to John.
- Knowing that John uses the Old Testament to explain what he is seeing and that a better understanding of the Old Testament will help us understand John and the Revelation.
- Understanding that not all of Revelation is in the future.
- And understanding the intermissions. The Revelation is not a linear timeline.

Symbolism

Another rule to follow should be to understand that The Revelation is full of symbolism. It is highly symbolic.

Debates rage between those who take the Revelation to be more literal than symbolic and those who take it to be more symbolic than literal. Are the stars actually stars, or are they comets, angels, or nuclear weapons? You already know where I stand. The stars are the host of heaven, the angels and demons, the unseen realm from our first rule. Sometimes you can't deny it. In Revelation 9:1, the star is given the keys to the bottomless pit. You don't give keys to stars or comets. Other times, it isn't clearly stated, but it is hard to picture the stars as anything other than spiritual beings.

> Revelation 12:3-4
>
> And another sign appeared in heaven: behold, a great red dragon, with seven heads and ten horns, and on his heads seven diadems. ⁴ His tail swept down a third of the stars of heaven and cast them to the earth.

Isn't it hard to picture Satan pulling down a third of the literal stars that are billions of miles away and much larger than our own planet? In fact, we are given a clue that John doesn't mean that at all. Satan's armies, also known as stars, are cast out of the sky a few verses later.

> Revelation 12:9

⁹ And the great dragon was thrown down, that ancient serpent, who is called the devil and Satan, the deceiver of the whole world—he was thrown down to the earth, and his angels were thrown down with him.

The stars Satan pulls down obviously represent his armies. Though it seems painfully obvious in chapter 12 there are other places where John leaves it open to interpretation. At least, it seems that way.

Revelation 8:10-11

¹⁰ The third angel blew his trumpet, and a great star fell from heaven, blazing like a torch, and it fell on a third of the rivers and on the springs of water. ¹¹ The name of the star is Wormwood. A third of the waters became wormwood, and many people died from the water, because it had been made bitter.

Is this a comet, a nuke, an angel? The answer is, I don't know. There is enough ambiguity that an honest person would need to leave it open for debate, but I lean toward a member of the unseen realm.

While people will argue over the meaning of stars and mountains falling from the sky, they rarely argue the dragons are literal. The dragon of chapter 12 is clearly Satan, 12:9 says as much, but what about chapter 13 and the beast? Is it a literal dragon? Is it a zoological creature? Of course not; it is symbolic.

> Revelation 13:1-3
>
> And I saw a beast rising out of the sea, with ten horns and seven heads, with ten diadems on its horns and blasphemous names on its heads. ² And the beast that I saw was like a leopard; its feet were like a bear's, and its mouth was like a lion's mouth. And to it, the dragon gave his power and his throne and great authority. ³ One of its heads seemed to have a mortal wound, but its mortal wound was healed, and the whole earth marveled as they followed the beast.

Many of you are already ahead of me, saying to yourself, "Oh, Oh, I know! It is the antichrist."

Okay. I agree, though John never says it.

Though we might agree, how is it that we come to a seven-headed dragon representing something that is opposed to Christ? And why is it that the beast looks like the dragon, both having seven heads and ten horns? The answer is because the dragon with seven heads represents anything that stands against God and his people and our second rule will be useful here. John knows his Old Testament and what he uses and how he uses it matters.

> Psalm 74:12-14

¹² Yet God my King is from of old, working salvation in the midst of the earth.

¹³ You divided the sea by your might; you broke the heads of the sea monsters on the waters.

¹⁴ You crushed the heads of Leviathan; you gave him as food for the creatures of the wilderness.

God crushed the heads of sea monsters and Leviathan. The Psalmist says that Leviathan had heads, in the plural. Never in the Bible, but in the literature of surrounding cultures, Leviathan is said to have seven heads. In ancient cultures Leviathan represents chaos. It represents anything that stands against order. In the Bible, to stand against order is to stand against God. Therefore, Leviathan is anti-God, or in New Testament language, an antichrist.

Leviathan is used to describe God's opponents. In Ezekiel 29 and 32, it is representing Pharoah and Egypt.

Ezekiel 29:3-5

"Behold, I am against you, Pharaoh king of Egypt, the great dragon that lies in the midst of his streams, that says, 'My Nile is my own; I made it for myself.'

⁴ I will put hooks in your jaws, and make the fish of your streams stick to your scales; and I will draw you up out

of the midst of your streams, with all the fish of your streams that stick to your scales.

⁵ And I will cast you out into the wilderness, you and all the fish of your streams; you shall fall on the open field, and not be brought together or gathered.

To the beasts of the earth and to the birds of the heavens, I give you as food.

Does that sound familiar? I will put a hook in your mouth and give you as food to the birds? It may to some. In a very popular chapter, Ezekiel 38, which is about the Gog/Magog war, we read:

> Ezekiel 38:3-4
>
> Behold, I am against you, O Gog, chief prince of Meshech and Tubal. ⁴ And I will turn you about and put hooks into your jaws, and I will bring you out, and all your army, horses and horsemen, all of them clothed in full armor, a great host...

And in Revelation 20:7-8...

> ⁷ And when the thousand years are ended, Satan will be released from his prison ⁸ and will come out to deceive the nations that are at the four corners of the earth, Gog and Magog, to gather them for battle; their number is like the sand of the sea.

Satan, who is described as a seven-headed dragon, is the hook God uses to bring his enemies, Gog of Magog, who is also described as a seven-headed sea monster, to battle. Satan is used to bring Leviathan to slaughter.

In Revelation 19, we read what happens to them.

Revelation 19:17-18

Then I saw an angel standing in the sun, and with a loud voice, he called to all the birds that fly directly overhead, "Come, gather for the great supper of God, [18] to eat the flesh of kings, the flesh of captains, the flesh of mighty men, the flesh of horses and their riders, and the flesh of all men, both free and slave, both small and great."

Remember that John uses the Old Testament to describe what he sees. The same thing happens to Leviathan in Ezekiel 29 that happens to the seven headed beast in Revelation 19. It happens in Psalm 74:14 and Ezekiel 39 as well.

In Revelation 12, John sees the dragon and calls him Satan, and in 13, he sees a beast come from the sea that looks like the dragon, but not exactly. It is obviously a second entity that is different and distinct from Satan. Isaiah mentions something similar.

Isaiah 27:1

> In that day the LORD, with his hard and great and strong sword, will punish Leviathan the fleeing serpent, Leviathan the twisting serpent, and he will slay the dragon that is in the sea.

Remember, Leviathan is a seven-headed dragon just like the one John describes. The Lord will punish Levithan, and he will slay the dragon. Isn't it amazing how it all fits together?

In Daniel 7, Daniel describes for us four beasts that represent four kingdoms. Their descriptions end up in the single beast of Revelation 13.

> Revelation 13:2
>
> And the beast that I saw was like a leopard; its feet were like a bear's, and its mouth was like a lion's mouth.

Here's the reference from Daniel 7:1-8 for comparison.

Daniel 7:1-8

> [1] In the first year of Belshazzar king of Babylon, Daniel saw a dream and visions of his head as he lay in his bed. Then he wrote down the dream and told the sum of the matter. [2] Daniel declared, "I saw in my vision by night, and behold, the four winds of heaven were stirring up the great sea. [3] And four great beasts came up out of the sea,

different from one another. ⁴ The first was like a lion and had eagles' wings. Then as I looked its wings were plucked off, and it was lifted up from the ground and made to stand on two feet like a man, and the mind of a man was given to it. ⁵ And behold, another beast, a second one, like a bear. It was raised up on one side. It had three ribs in its mouth between its teeth; and it was told, 'Arise, devour much flesh.' ⁶ After this I looked, and behold, another, like a leopard, with four wings of a bird on its back. And the beast had four heads, and dominion was given to it. ⁷ After this I saw in the night visions, and behold, a fourth beast, terrifying and dreadful and exceedingly strong. It had great iron teeth; it devoured and broke in pieces and stamped what was left with its feet. It was different from all the beasts that were before it, and it had ten horns. ⁸ I considered the horns, and behold, there came up among them another horn, a little one, before which three of the first horns were plucked up by the roots. And behold, in this horn were eyes like the eyes of a man, and a mouth speaking great things. [5]

You simply cannot deny that the four beasts of Daniel 7 become the single beast of Revelation 13.

---

[5] *The Holy Bible: English Standard Version* (Wheaton, IL: Crossway Bibles, 2016), Da 7:1–8.

Why does John do this? Why does the dragon and the beast match the symbolic description of the Pharaoh and Egypt from Ezekiel? Why does John's dragon and beast sound like Isaiah's Leviathan and dragon from the sea? Why does John's beast in Revelation 13 look like a hybrid of the four beasts of Daniel 7?

Because they represent the enemies of God. They represent all things anti-God. They represent all things antichrist. Not a single man, but all men who align themselves with the fallen elohim, the beasts. I don't believe Revelation 13 is symbolic of a man who will come and fight against God and his people. Rather, it represents the system of our enemy that has, does, and will continue to fight against anything and anyone that aligns itself with the God of heaven. It has been this way since the garden.

Paul called it the course of this world, Ephesians 2:1 and identified it as the spirit that is "*NOW*" at work in the sons of disobedience. In Ephesians 6, he says, "*Put on the whole armor of God, that you may be able to stand against the schemes of the devil.*" He then goes on to describe the whole of the unseen power structure. "*rulers...authorities...cosmic powers over this present darkness...spiritual forces in heavenly places.*"

John says it is the love of this world.

1 John 2:15-18

¹⁵ Do not love the world or the things in the world. If anyone loves the world, the love of the Father is not in him. ¹⁶ For all that is in the world–the desires of the flesh and the desires of the eyes and pride of life–Is not from the Father but is from the world. ¹⁷ And the world is passing away along with its desires, but whoever does the will of God abides forever.

He directly relates the love of this world to the appearance of antichrists in the next verse.

¹⁸ Children, it is the last hour, and as you have heard that the antichrist is coming, so now many antichrists have come. Therefore, we know that it is the last hour.

The love of this world had caused many to leave their fellowship. There is so much here but I don't have the space to cover it all, but notice two things.

1. John says, "*We know that it is the last hour.*" Sounds like "*soon*" and "*the time is near*" from Revelation 1. I'll return briefly to that at the close of this chapter.
2. John says, "*You have heard the antichrist is coming so, many are now here.*"

Are we sitting around waiting for something that is already here? Are we waiting for the right world leader to come along and show himself as the leader of the one world government that everyone will follow while John is screaming to us that the system of our enemy is in place, and it is the love of this world by which he deceives us?

I think so. I think we are waiting for something that is in our pockets. In our entertainment, in our schools, in the stores we shop at, and in our cabinets at home, and in our subscriptions. it's in our eyes and in our ears.

John says it even more clearly in 1 John 4.

> 1 John 4:1-3
>
> Beloved, do not believe every spirit, but test the spirits to see whether they are from God, for many false prophets have gone out into the world. [2] By this you know the Spirit of God: every spirit that confesses that Jesus Christ has come in the flesh is from God, [3] and every spirit that does not confess Jesus is not from God. This is the spirit of the antichrist, which you heard was coming and now is in the world already.

The spirit of antichrist is alive and well and has been since John's time, and many people have fully embraced it. Many already carry the mark.

The last rule is...

The Revelation is Highly Practical.

Revelation 13:16-18

¹⁶ Also, it causes all, both small and great, both rich and poor, both free and slave, to be marked on the right hand or the forehead, ¹⁷ so that no one can buy or sell unless he has the mark, that is, the name of the beast or the number of its name. ¹⁸ This calls for wisdom: let the one who has understanding calculate the number of the beast, for it is the number of a man, and his number is 666.

I want you to know that I understand the next bit of information will be different from anything you've read or heard before, but I want you to prayerfully consider it. We are told to *calculate the number of the beast*. Calculate means to count or to add up. The word "*number*" used here by John is used 18 times in the New Testament, and everywhere else, it is used to describe counting the number of men or of angels as in a census.

Here are a few examples:

John 6:10

¹⁰ Jesus said, "Have the people sit down." Now, there was much grass in the place. **So the men sat down, about five thousand in number.**

Acts 4:4

⁴ But many of those who had heard the word believed, and **the number of the men came to about five thousand.**

Revelation 7:4

⁴ And I heard **the number of the sealed, 144,000,** sealed from every tribe of the sons of Israel:

Instead of looking for a clever way to use 666 to figure out who the antichrist will be, realizing that John tells us the antichrist was alive and well in his day and it was called the spirit of the antichrist, and considering the definition of the word "number" as it is used everywhere else in the New Testament, maybe we should look at an alternative to understanding the meaning of 666. Maybe we should look to the Old Testament for a clue. Remember our second rule: John knows his Old Testament and uses it.

Zechariah 13:7-9

⁷ "Awake, O sword, against my shepherd, against the man who stands next to me," declares the LORD of hosts. "Strike the shepherd, and the sheep will be scattered; I will turn my hand against the little ones.

⁸ In the whole land, declares the LORD, two thirds shall be cut off and perish, and one third shall be left alive.

⁹ And I will put this third into the fire, and refine them as one refines silver, and test them as gold is tested. They will call upon my name, and I will answer them. I will say, 'They are my 'people' ; and they will say, 'The LORD is my God.'"

Did you notice it? Do you notice two-thirds shall be cut off, and one-third shall remain and that third will be tried by fire, and God will call them, *my people*?

Sixty-six, six is two-thirds or 66.6. Maybe John is trying to tell us that about two-thirds of humanity will reject the God of heaven and choose to follow the beast, the system of the antichrist, the love of this world.

Matthew 7:13-14

¹³ "Enter by the narrow gate. For the gate is wide, and the way is easy that leads to destruction, and those who enter by it are many. ¹⁴ For the gate is narrow and the way is hard that leads to life, and those who find it are few.

Jesus hints at such an interpretation in Matthew 24

Matthew 24:11-12

¹¹ And many false prophets will arise and lead many astray. ¹² And because lawlessness will be increased, the love of many will grow cold.

What is a false prophet but an antichrist? A false prophet is one who opposes the work of God. But what of the mark? Consider that it might be image-bearing.

We are created to be the image of God. Not to look like him but to represent him to the world. We carry his name. When God says *thou shall not take my name in vain*, he isn't telling us not to swear. Rather, he is telling us not to say we belong to God while living like we belong to the beast. We are to image his love to the world around us.

What do you image?

In Ezekiel 9, we are told that God calls his angels to go through the city and strike those who have sinned against him. Before he releases them to do it, he sends another through the city to mark some. This angel is told, *"Pass through the city, through Jerusalem, and put a mark on the foreheads of the men who sigh and groan over all the abominations that are committed in it."*

Would God seal you as one of his? Do you sigh and groan over sin? Do injustices bother you? Or have you taken his name in vain? God said of Israel, *"My name is profaned among the nations because of you."* They had taken his name in vain. They failed to represent him well among the nations. They were imaging something else.

What do you image?

I want to suggest that John is not describing a man who will force the masses to stand in line and announce their allegiance by receiving a mark or a chip. Rather, John is asking us to take up that choice today. To place upon ourselves the mandate of nonparticipation. This was happening in the first century. The church had come out of a world filled with idolatry and the worship of other gods. They elected to care for one another and to not participate in the feasts with foods sacrificed to idols and all kinds of sexual immoralities. They chose to remove themselves from the things that had and would ensnare them. They chose to face death and exile for the name of Christ. This is something that has happened, will happen, and something that does happen today. We as believers should be participating, or not participating, whether it is forced or not.

Are you sealed, part of the one-third, or are you marked as part of the two-thirds? Whose image do you carry?

I want to encourage you today to choose the name of God. Choose to image him and represent him well, and he will seal you. But, of course, you can choose to be marked and image the world, which is the beast, the antichrist.

The Beast Has A Name: Gog

One of the rules to understand The Revelation is knowing that John is familiar with his Bible and uses it to help him explain what he is seeing. Another rule is understanding recapitulation. John is not writing a linear chronology from start to finish. John is unfolding the Revelation like a play writer using acts to tell the whole story. Like a play, John retells the story in varying degrees to fill in details and introduce new characters. All the acts together tell a complete story. The following will help you see these two rules for understanding the Revelation in action.

First, John draws heavily upon Ezekiel 38-39 to describe the battle he witnesses. These chapters describe the battle of Gog of Magog. If you are not familiar with it, stop to read it. Many of its details are important when trying to understand the Revelation.

Second, John unfolds the battle over four acts.

The four acts of Revelation are:

Act 1: Revelation 4-11

Act 2: Revelation 12-16

Act 3: Revelation 17-19

Act 4: Revelation 20

Each of these four divisions, these four acts, tell the same story with new details, events, or characters, but they also have repeating details, events, and characters. One of the repeating events is a great battle. This battle is found in each act in the following passages:

Act 1: Revelation 9, 11:7-8

Act 2: Revelation 14:17-20, Revelation 16:13-16.

Act 3: Revelation 19:11-21

Act 4: Revelation 20:7-10

By connecting Revelation's four battles to the single battle prophesied by Ezekiel in Chapters 38-39, we are connecting them together, showing John's use of recapitulation. Each of the four battles we see in Revelation connect separately to Ezekiel 38-39 and therefore prove that they are separate descriptions of the same battle. Again, John is not describing four separate battles. He is describing the battle of Gog and Magog over four acts. Each time, he provides more details like location and characters.

Are you ready to see how this works?

Ezekiel 38:1-6

[1] The word of the LORD came to me: [2] "Son of man, set your face toward Gog, of the land of Magog, the chief prince of Meshech and Tubal, and prophesy against

him ³ and say, Thus says the Lord GOD: Behold, I am against you, O Gog, chief prince of Meshech and Tubal. ⁴ And **I will turn you about and put hooks into your jaws, and I will bring you out**, and all your army, horses and horsemen, all of them clothed in full armor, a great host, all of them with buckler and shield, wielding swords. ⁵ **Persia, Cush, and Put are with them, all of them with shield and helmet;** ⁶ **Gomer and all his hordes; Beth-togarmah from the uttermost parts of the north with all his hordes— many peoples are with you**.

Now compare that passage to Revelation 20:7-8

Revelation 20:7-8

⁷ And when the thousand years are ended, **Satan will be released from his prison** ⁸ **and will come out to deceive the nations that are at the four corners of the earth**, Gog and Magog, to gather them for battle; their number is like the sand of the sea.

John presents Satan as the hook in the Jaw of Gog from Ezekiel 38:4 that God uses to draw out the nations that are at the four corners. The four corners simply represent the four directions, using Israel as the center of the action. Ezekiel does the same thing using the names of the nations in the four directions. Beth-togarmah is in the North, Persia is to the west,

Cush is to the south, and Put is to the east of Israel. John doesn't use the names because they aren't relevant to what will happen. The nations at the four corners simply means all nations. All of them will come against Israel when God uses Satan as a hook to draw them out. ALL NATIONS.

This gathering of nations at the battle of Gog/Magog is repeated throughout the Revelation and is found in all four acts. Revelation 20:7-8 is found in Act 4. Then…

Revelation 19:19 from Act 3 says…

> [19] And I saw the beast and the kings of the earth with their armies gathered to make war against him who was sitting on the horse and against his army.

Revelation 16:13-14 from Act 2 states…

> [13] And I saw, coming out of the mouth of the dragon and out of the mouth of the beast and out of the mouth of the false prophet, three unclean spirits like frogs. [14] For they are demonic spirits, performing signs, who go abroad to the kings of the whole world, to assemble them for battle on the great day of God the Almighty.

Rev 11:7-9 from the first acts says…

> [7] And when they have finished their testimony, the beast that rises from the bottomless pit will make war on them and conquer them and kill them, [8] and their

dead bodies will lie in the street of the great city that symbolically is called Sodom and Egypt, where their Lord was crucified. ⁹ For three and a half days, some from the peoples and tribes and languages and nations will gaze at their dead bodies and refuse to let them be placed in a tomb...

(See also Revelation 9:1, 11; 14:17-19)

Like the Gog Magog war, the battles described in Revelation included nations from the four corners, which simply means all nations. What I hope you are catching is the idea that John is not describing four separate battles. He is describing a single battle four times. Try to see the things that are repeated and how they connect to what you read in Ezekiel.

Gathered and Counted

Let's keep reading from Ezekiel. This is God speaking to Gog.

Ezekiel 38:7-8

⁷ "Be ready and keep ready, you and all your hosts that are assembled about you, and be a guard for them. ⁸ After many days, you will be mustered. In the latter years, you will go against the land that is restored from war...

In Revelation 20:1-3 Satan is bound in chains in the bottomless pit for 1000 years. After 1000 years, he is released as described in Revelation 20:7-8. The purpose of his release is to gather the armies of Gog. Satan is the hook that God uses to draw the nations, Gog, to Israel (I will explain that more in a bit). One thousand is defined by The Jewish Annotated New Testament as "a sufficient enormity."[6] Others describe 1000 years as being a metaphor for, "a long time." Ezekiel 38:8 reads, "After a long time, you shall be summoned."[7] After a long time, which John describes as 1000 years, Satan will be called upon to be a hook in Gog's mouth and draw the nations to Israel for judgment.[8]

Ezekiel tells us the hosts with Gog will be mustered. The word mustered means gathered and/or counted.[9] Look at Revelation 9:16

> Revelation 9:16
>
> [16] The number of mounted troops was twice ten thousand times ten thousand; I heard their number.

John numbers what Ezekiel says will be gathered at two hundred million. Also, what Ezekiel says will be after a long

---

[6] The Jewish Annotated New Testament, Second Edition, Oxford 2017, The Numerology of Revelation, Page 550.
[7] The Jewish Study Bible, Second Edition, JPS, Oxford 2014, Ezekiel 38:8.
[8] This is argued in greater detail elsewhere so time to do it here was not taken.
[9] 7212 פָּקַד (pā·qăḏ): v.; ≡ Str 6485; TWOT 1802—1. LN 60.1–60.9 (qal) count, number, inventory, take stock, i.e., use numbers to determine a quantity of objects (Nu 1:19). Dictionary of Biblical Languages, Hebrew.

time, John says will be 1,000 years, and I believe John is employing hyperbole. One thousand years is a sufficient enormity. It means, in essence, as long as it takes.

The point here is to continue to make connections.

The Land

> Ezekiel 38:8
>
> After many days, you will be mustered. In the latter years, you will go against the land that is restored from war, the land whose people were gathered from many peoples upon the mountains of Israel, which had been a continual waste. Its people were brought out from the peoples and now dwell securely, all of them.

The land where people dwell securely is Israel. That is clear from the context that Ezekiel 36 and 37 provides.

> Ezekiel 37:21-22
>
> "Thus says the Lord GOD: Behold, I will take the people of Israel from the nations among which they have gone, and will gather them from all around, and bring them to their own land. [22] And I will make them one nation in the land, on the mountains of Israel."

Ezekiel describes the nations being gathered against Israel and John clearly identifies the gathering place as Jerusalem.

Revelation 11:8 (Act 1) John says...

> and their dead bodies will lie in the street of the great city that symbolically is called Sodom and Egypt, where their Lord was crucified.

In Act 2, Revelation 16:14-16, John says...

> [14] For they are demonic spirits, performing signs, who go abroad to the kings of the whole world, to assemble them for battle on the great day of God the Almighty. [15] ("Behold, I am coming like a thief! Blessed is the one who stays awake, keeping his garments on, that he may not go about naked and be seen exposed!") [16] And they assembled them at the place that in Hebrew is called Armageddon.

We have talked about Armageddon before. It should be translated "Mountain of God," which would mean Jerusalem, Mount Zion.

In Act 4, Revelation 20:9, John says...

> [9] And they marched up over the broad plain of the earth and surrounded the camp of the saints and the beloved city, but fire came down from heaven and consumed them...

Ezekiel is describing the return of the Jewish exiles from the nations to Israel. Something that is happening today. In

1948, Israel became a nation again, and every year, more Jews from all over the world return home. When they are safely in their land, God will use Satan to gather the nations against Israel. Why? To consume them. God is going to judge the nations.

The Storm

Ezekiel describes this evil alliance of nations coming against Israel as a storm.

> Ezekiel 38:9
>
> [9] You will advance, coming on like a storm. You will be like a cloud covering the land, you and all your hordes, and many peoples with you.

In Revelation 9:1-2 John describes the army that arises from the bottomless pit coming out like smoke from a furnace so that the sun and the air were darkened, like storm clouds.

The Hook

In Ezekiel 38:4, Gog is pulled into battle with a hook. I've already connected this to the deception that draws the nations into battle. This is confirmed by Ezekiel 38:10.

> Ezekiel 38:10

¹⁰ "Thus says the Lord GOD: On that day, thoughts will come into your mind, and you will devise an evil scheme...

Here's how John says it.

Revelation 16:12-14

¹² The sixth angel poured out his bowl on the great river Euphrates, and its water was dried up, to prepare the way for the kings from the east. ¹³ And I saw, coming out of the mouth of the dragon and out of the mouth of the beast and out of the mouth of the false prophet, three unclean spirits like frogs. ¹⁴ For they are demonic spirits, performing signs, who go abroad to the kings of the whole world, to assemble them for battle on the great day of God the Almighty.

At God's command, Satan devises the evil scheme to bring the nations to Israel. Ultimately, Satan is the tool. He is the hook that God uses to draw out Gog. By deception of signs, Satan convinces Gog he can win. Gog devises a plan. Gog is the power behind the nations, the unseen enemies of God. (See Page 13)

Babylon

Notice what Ezekiel says about those who come against Israel.

Ezekiel 38:11-13

> ...¹¹ and say, 'I will go up against the land of unwalled villages. I will fall upon the quiet people who dwell securely, all of them dwelling without walls, and having no bars or gates,' ¹² to seize spoil and carry off plunder, to turn your hand against the waste places that are now inhabited, and the people who were gathered from the nations, who have acquired livestock and goods, who dwell at the center of the earth. ¹³ Sheba and Dedan and the merchants of Tarshish and all its leaders will say to you, 'Have you come to seize spoil? Have you assembled your hosts to carry off plunder, to carry away silver and gold, to take away livestock and goods, to seize great spoil?'

This passage has clear similarities to John's passage concerning Babylon.

Revelation 18:11-20

> ¹¹ And the merchants of the earth weep and mourn for her, since no one buys their cargo anymore, ¹² cargo of gold, silver, jewels, pearls, fine linen, purple cloth, silk, scarlet cloth, all kinds of scented wood, all kinds of articles of ivory, all kinds of articles of costly wood, bronze, iron and marble, ¹³ cinnamon, spice, incense, myrrh, frankincense, wine, oil, fine flour, wheat, cattle

and sheep, horses and chariots, and slaves, that is, human souls.

¹⁴ "The fruit for which your soul longed has gone from you, and all your delicacies and your splendors are lost to you, never to be found again!"

¹⁵ The merchants of these wares, who gained wealth from her, will stand far off, in fear of her torment, weeping and mourning aloud,

¹⁶ "Alas, alas, for the great city that was clothed in fine linen, in purple and scarlet, adorned with gold, with jewels, and with pearls!

¹⁷ For in a single hour, all this wealth has been laid waste."

And all shipmasters and seafaring men, sailors and all whose trade is on the sea, stood far off ¹⁸ and cried out as they saw the smoke of her burning,

"What city was like the great city?"

¹⁹ And they threw dust on their heads as they wept and mourned, crying out, "Alas, alas, for the great city where all who had ships at sea grew rich by her wealth! For in a single hour, she has been laid waste.

²⁰ Rejoice over her, O heaven, and you saints and apostles and prophets, for God has given judgment for you against her!"

The merchants in Ezekiel are concerned about the implications of what they see will come to pass, while the merchants in Revelation 18 witness the devastation. The fears of Ezekiel's merchants have become the realities of John's merchants.

The Horses

Let's look at the horses from Ezekiel 38 and Revelation 9.

Ezekiel 38:14-16

¹⁴ "Therefore, son of man, prophesy, and say to Gog, Thus says the Lord GOD: On that day when my people Israel are dwelling securely, will you not know it? ¹⁵ You will come from your place out of the uttermost parts of the north, you and many peoples with you, **all of them riding on horses, a great host, a mighty army.** ¹⁶ You will come up against my people, Israel, like a cloud covering the land. In the latter days, I will bring you against my land, that the nations may know me, when through you, O Gog, I vindicate my holiness before their eyes.

We've related the smoke that arises from the bottomless pit in Revelation 9:1-2 to the storm cloud on the land above, but in the same chapter, the army is described as horses prepared for battle.

Revelation 9:7-9

⁷ In appearance, the locusts were like horses prepared for battle: on their heads were what looked like crowns of gold; their faces were like human faces, ⁸ their hair like women's hair, and their teeth like lions' teeth; ⁹ they had breastplates like breastplates of iron, and the noise of their wings was like the noise of **many chariots with horses rushing into battle**.

John describes a great army rushing into battle on many chariots with horses while Ezekiel sees a great host, a mighty army, riding on horses.

The Great Earthquake

Both men describe a great earthquake.

Ezekiel 38:17-20

¹⁷ "Thus says the Lord GOD: Are you he of whom I spoke in former days by my servants the prophets of Israel, who in those days prophesied for years that I would bring you against them? ¹⁸ But on that day, the day that Gog shall come against the land of Israel,

declares the Lord GOD, my wrath will be roused in my anger. ¹⁹ For in my jealousy and in my blazing wrath I declare, **On that day there shall be a great earthquake in the land of Israel**. ²⁰ The fish of the sea and the birds of the heavens and the beasts of the field and all creeping things that creep on the ground, and all the people who are on the face of the earth, shall quake at my presence. And the mountains shall be thrown down, and the cliffs shall fall, and every wall shall tumble to the ground.

The great earthquake is represented in several places. It is associated with the war against the two witnesses in Revelation 11.

Revelation 11:19

¹⁹ Then God's temple in heaven was opened, and the ark of his covenant was seen within his temple. There were flashes of lightning, rumblings, peals of thunder, **an earthquake**, and heavy hail.

It is associated with the war of Revelation 14:17-20, which John details in the closing passages of Chapter 16.

Revelation 16:18-21

¹⁸ And there were flashes of lightning, rumblings, peals of thunder, **and a great earthquake** such as there had never been since man was on the earth, so great was

that earthquake. ⁱ⁹ The great city was split into three parts, and the cities of the nations fell, and God remembered Babylon the great, to make her drain the cup of the wine of the fury of his wrath. ²⁰ And every island fled away, and no mountains were to be found. ²¹ And great hailstones, about one hundred pounds each, fell from heaven on people; and they cursed God for the plague of the hail, because the plague was so severe.

Notice the familiar wording from Revelation 11:19 in Revelation 16:18 and 16:21, Verse 18 says, *"And there were flashes of lightning, peals of thunder, and a great earthquake."* Verse 21 states, *"and great hailstones."* He does this because Chapter 11 and Chapters 14 (verses 17-20) and 16 (verses 18-21) are the same event: the Gog/Magog war of Ezekiel 38-39.

The Sword

Both men are going to talk about a sword coming against Gog to destroy him and his armies.

Ezekiel 38:21-23

²¹ **I will summon a sword against Gog on all my mountains**, declares the Lord God. Every man's sword will be against his brother. ²² With pestilence and

bloodshed, I will enter into judgment with him, and I will rain upon him and his hordes and the many peoples who are with him torrential rains and hailstones, fire, and sulfur. ²³ So I will show my greatness and my holiness and make myself known in the eyes of many nations. Then they will know that I am the LORD.

John describes this sword as belonging to him, who is called *Faithful and True*.

Revelation 19:11-17

¹¹ Then I saw heaven opened, and behold, a white horse! The one sitting on it is called Faithful and True, and in righteousness, he judges and makes war. ¹² His eyes are like a flame of fire, and on his head are many diadems, and he has a name written that no one knows but himself. ¹³ He is clothed in a robe dipped in blood, and the name by which he is called is The Word of God. ¹⁴ And the armies of heaven, arrayed in fine linen, white and pure, were following him on white horses. ¹⁵ **From his mouth comes a sharp sword with which to strike down the nations**, and he will rule them with a rod of iron. He will tread the winepress of the fury of the wrath of God the Almighty. ¹⁶ On his robe and on his thigh, he has a name written, King of kings and Lord of lords.

The rider on the white horse is the sword summoned against the armies of Gog. Furthermore, God rains fire upon them to consume them as promised by Ezekiel. Notice also John's use of the winepress in chapter 19, *"He will tread the winepress of the fury of the wrath of God the Almighty."* That should be familiar because the winepress is presented in Act 2, Revelation 14:17-20.

> Revelation 14:17-20
>
> [17] Then another angel came out of the temple in heaven, and he too had a sharp sickle. [18] And another angel came out from the altar, the angel who has authority over the fire, and he called with a loud voice to the one who had the sharp sickle, "Put in your sickle and gather the clusters from the vine of the earth, for its grapes are ripe." [19] So the angel swung his sickle across the earth and gathered the grape harvest of the earth **and threw it into the great winepress of the wrath of God**. [20] And the winepress was trodden outside the city, and blood flowed from the winepress, as high as a horse's bridle, for 1,600 stadia.

These aren't different battles. Ezekiel and John are describing the same battle. John is doing it in small releases over several acts.

Notice also that John describes fire raining down just as Ezekiel did in Ezekiel 38:22

> Revelation 20:9
>
> ⁹ And they marched up over the broad plain of the earth and surrounded the camp of the saints and the beloved city, **but fire came down from heaven** and consumed them...

Again, these are not different battles. Revelation 11, 14, 16, 19 and 20 are all describing the battle of Gog and Magog.

The Feast

> Ezekiel 39:1-6
>
> 39 "And you, son of man, prophesy against Gog and say, Thus says the Lord GOD: Behold, I am against you, O Gog, chief prince of Meshech and Tubal. ² And I will turn you about and drive you forward, and bring you up from the uttermost parts of the north, and lead you against the mountains of Israel. ³ Then I will strike your bow from your left hand, and will make your arrows drop out of your right hand. ⁴ You shall fall on the mountains of Israel, you and all your hordes and the peoples who are with you. **I will give you to birds of prey of every sort and to the beasts of the field to be devoured.** ⁵ You shall fall in the open field, for I

have spoken, declares the Lord GOD. **⁶ I will send fire on Magog and on those who dwell securely in the coastlands**, and they shall know that I am the LORD.

We don't need to revisit the fire falling on the armies gathered against Israel in Revelation 20:9, but the war of Chapter 19 connects nicely to Ezekiel 39:4 because John describes an angel calling the birds of the air to come feast on the armies of the beast. We will see it again below and address it more fully there.

Ezekiel 39:7-20

⁷ "And my holy name I will make known in the midst of my people Israel, and I will not let my holy name be profaned anymore. And the nations shall know that I am the LORD, the Holy One in Israel. ⁸ Behold, it is coming, and it will be brought about, declares the Lord GOD. That is the day of which I have spoken.

⁹ "Then those who dwell in the cities of Israel will go out and make fires of the weapons and burn them, shields and bucklers, bow and arrows, clubs and spears; and they will make fires of them for seven years, ¹⁰ so that they will not need to take wood out of the field or cut down any out of the forests, for they will make their fires of the weapons. They will seize the spoil of those who

despoiled them, and plunder those who plundered them, declares the Lord GOD.

¹¹ "On that day I will give to Gog a place for burial in Israel, the Valley of the Travelers, east of the sea. It will block the travelers, for there, Gog and all his multitude will be buried. It will be called the Valley of Hamon-gog. ¹² For seven months, the house of Israel will be burying them in order to cleanse the land. ¹³ All the people of the land will bury them, and it will bring them renown on the day that I show my glory, declares the Lord GOD. ¹⁴ They will set apart men to travel through the land regularly and bury those travelers remaining on the face of the land, so as to cleanse it. At the end of seven months, they will make their search. ¹⁵ And when these travel through the land, and anyone sees a human bone, then he shall set up a sign by it, till the buriers have buried it in the Valley of Hamon-gog. ¹⁶ (Hamonah is also the name of the city.) Thus shall they cleanse the land.

¹⁷ "As for you, son of man, thus says the Lord GOD: **Speak to the birds of every sort and to all beasts of the field: 'Assemble and come, gather from all around to the sacrificial feast that I am preparing for you, a great sacrificial feast on the mountains of Israel, and you shall eat flesh and drink blood.** ¹⁸

You shall eat the flesh of the mighty, and drink the blood of the princes of the earth—of rams, of lambs, and of he-goats, of bulls, all of them fat beasts of Bashan. [19] And you shall eat fat till you are filled, and drink blood till you are drunk, at the sacrificial feast that I am preparing for you. [20] And you shall be filled at my table with horses and charioteers, with mighty men and all kinds of warriors,' declares the Lord God.

Here, Ezekiel revisits the feast that is prepared for the birds of the air and the beast of the field from Verse 4 above. They will feast on the armies of Gog. Again, John details the same event in Revelation 19.

Revelation 19:17-21

[17] Then I saw an angel standing in the sun, and with a loud voice, **he called to all the birds that fly directly overhead, "Come, gather for the great supper of God, [18] to eat the flesh of kings, the flesh of captains, the flesh of mighty men, the flesh of horses and their riders, and the flesh of all men, both free and slave, both small and great."** [19] And I saw the beast and the kings of the earth with their armies gathered to make war against him who was sitting on the horse and against his army. [20] And the

beast was captured, and with it the false prophet who in its presence had done the signs by which he deceived those who had received the mark of the beast and those who worshiped its image. These two were thrown alive into the lake of fire that burns with sulfur. [21] And the rest were slain by the sword that came from the mouth of him who was sitting on the horse, and all the birds were gorged with their flesh.

The connection between Ezekiel 39 and Revelation 19 is clear, but there is another connection between the Gog/Magog war and John's Revelation that this feast makes that is not so clear. Talking about it will help us make a connection I have made more than once above. Gog represents the spiritual powers that Satan deceives into driving the human armies against Israel.

Leviathan

In Psalm 74, Leviathan is given as food for the creatures of the wilderness. Speaking of God, the psalmist says,

> [13] You divided the sea by your might; you broke the heads of the sea monsters on the waters. [14] You crushed the heads of Leviathan; you gave him as food for the creatures of the wilderness.

The psalmist uses "heads" (plural) to describe Leviathan. Never in the Bible, but in other ancient literature, Leviathan is said to have seven heads. I mentioned this in an earlier chapter. It doesn't take much to make the connection to John's seven-headed dragon and the seven-headed beast of Revelation 12, 13, and even 17. The beast that rises from the bottomless pit in Revelation 9:1-2, 11, and 11:7 is described as a seven-headed beast in chapter 17:7-8.

How can we know this?

In Revelation 9:11 we are told the army that ascends from the bottomless pit has a king over them. His name is Abaddon in Hebrew and Apollyon in Greek. Abaddon means destruction, and Apollyon means destroyer. In Revelation 17 the beast is described as having seven heads, 10 horns and he is about to rise from the bottomless pit and go to destruction. The connections are quite clear. The head of the army that ascends out of the pit and brings the armies of the world against Israel is the seven-headed beast of Revelation 17. This beast of chapter 17 is Satan, the dragon from Revelation 12. John clearly identifies him in Rev 20 as going into the pit and then experiencing destruction in the Lake of Fire.

Revelation 20:1-3

20 Then I saw an angel coming down from heaven, holding in his hand the key to the bottomless pit and a great chain. ² And he seized the dragon, that ancient

serpent, who is the devil and Satan, and bound him for a thousand years, ³ and threw him into the pit, and shut it and sealed it over him, so that he might not deceive the nations any longer, until the thousand years were ended. After that, he must be released for a little while.

Revelation 20:7-10

⁷ And when the thousand years are ended, Satan will be released from his prison ⁸ and will come out to deceive the nations that are at the four corners of the earth, Gog and Magog, to gather them for battle; their number is like the sand of the sea. ⁹ And they marched up over the broad plain of the earth and surrounded the camp of the saints and the beloved city, but fire came down from heaven and consumed them, ¹⁰ and the devil who had deceived them was thrown into the lake of fire and sulfur where the beast and the false prophet were, and they will be tormented day and night forever and ever.

Both Satan and Gog are described as Leviathan/Chaos creatures.

Leviathan is described in ancient literature just as John has described him, and he is connected to Gog because they are both given to the creatures of the earth for food, but there is one more minor connection that I think should be made. In the opening verses of Ezekiel 38, God says through the prophet to Gog, "*I will turn you about and put hooks into your jaws, and I will bring you out.*" Earlier, we connected the hook to Satan, who is released from the bottomless pit to draw the nations to Israel for judgment. That leaves the seven-headed beasts of chapter 13 to represent Gog and his armies from the four corners representing all the nations of the world. The connection to Leviathan is made in Job 41.

Job 41:1-2

[1] "Can you draw out **Leviathan** with a fishhook or press down his tongue with a cord? [2] **Can you put a rope in his nose or pierce his jaw with a hook?**

Speaking to Job, God asks, "*Can you pierce the jaw of Leviathan with a hook?*" The obvious answer from Job is no, but equally as obvious is that God can. God can and will put a hook in the mouth of Leviathan, who Ezekiel calls Gog and John calls the Beast, and bring him out along with his allies to the land of Israel to be judged.

Ezekiel 39:21-29

[21] "And I will set my glory among the nations, and all the nations shall see my judgment that I have executed, and my hand that I have laid on them. [22] The house of Israel shall know that I am the LORD their God, from that

day forward. ²³ And the nations shall know that the house of Israel went into captivity for their iniquity, because they dealt so treacherously with me that I hid my face from them and gave them into the hand of their adversaries, and they all fell by the sword. ²⁴ I dealt with them according to their uncleanness and their transgressions and hid my face from them.

²⁵ "Therefore thus says the Lord GOD: Now I will restore the fortunes of Jacob and have mercy on the whole house of Israel, and I will be jealous for my holy name. ²⁶ They shall forget their shame and all the treachery they have practiced against me, when they dwell securely in their land with none to make them afraid, ²⁷ when I have brought them back from the peoples and gathered them from their enemies' lands, and through them have vindicated my holiness in the sight of many nations. ²⁸ Then they shall know that I am the LORD their God, because I sent them into exile among the nations and then assembled them into their own land. I will leave none of them remaining among the nations anymore. ²⁹ And I will not hide my face any more from them, when I pour out my Spirit upon the house of Israel, declares the Lord GOD." (ESV)

The battles described in Revelation 9-11; 14:17 through Chapter 16; Chapter 18; Chapter 19:11-21 and finally 20:7-10 are the same battle, and they are all the Gog/Magog war of Ezekiel 38-39 based on the connections I have made above.

The Temple

The purpose of this chapter was to connect Ezekiel 38-39 to the battles of Revelation, but there is another connection that I want to briefly make. Ezekiel continues in chapters 40-48 to describe the temple and life after the destruction of Gog. I won't take the time to describe it in detail, but it is like Eden. What Ezekiel does in detail in chapter 40-48 John summarizes in Revelation 21-22 by speaking of the new Jerusalem coming down from heaven. There are differences, but there are obvious connections that tell us that John and Ezekiel are seeing the same events. It is my opinion that to understand the Revelation, we need to fill our mind with what filled John's, the Old Testament. Time and time again, he pulls from his Bible to help him describe what he is seeing in the vision. Job's description of Leviathan being led around by a hook in his mouth, the psalmist's description of the multi-headed Leviathan's defeat and being given over to the creatures for food, the battle of Gog, and Ezekiel's description of the temple all informs the reader concerning John's Revelation.

Conclusion

The purpose of this and the following chapter is to fully lay out how the rules I have presented play out as we read our Bibles. John knows his Bible and if we want to understand him, we need to know it, too. (Rule #2) The Old Testament is important, and if you want to be a serious student of the Word, you need to become familiar with it.

I have also laid out how the Recapitulation Rule works. John is not describing four battles but a single great battle that he lays out over several retellings of the story. Each of the acts (1-4) should be stacked on top of each other rather than following each other on the timeline.

> Revelation 1-3; Revelation 4-11; Revelation 21-22
>
> Revelation 12-16
>
> Revelation 17-19
>
> Revelation 20

At the end of each act, realize that you have just heard the whole story. It may not provide all the details, but it contained a beginning and an end. It isn't until you've read all four acts that you have all the necessary information, but you've heard the story from beginning to end, nevertheless.

Let's continue to apply the rules by taking a look at the Tribulation.

Welcome To The Tribulation

The Greek word θλῖψις (*thlipsis*) is translated "tribulation" 17 times by the ESV. It is often associated with a future seven-year period of tribulation that will come upon the whole world in the last days, though it is never explicitly associated with a seven-year period in scripture. Many commentators believe John's Revelation describes this future seven-year tribulation, but John uses the word five times in Revelation and each time he does, he is describing current situations. Once calling himself a partner in tribulation, three times about the churches in Asia whom he is addressing the letter to, and one time of those "coming" out of the great tribulation in Revelation 7. The verb "coming" is a present tense verb and indicates continuing action or something that is in the process of happening. How is it then that we come to this idea of a future seven-year tribulation?

This idea of a seven-year tribulation comes from Daniel 9. There, we find Daniel, who has been exiled to Babylon, reading a letter from Jeremiah, his contemporary and fellow prophet. (I should note that not everyone considers Daniel a prophet.)

Daniel 9:1-2

9 In the first year of Darius the son of Ahasuerus, by descent a Mede, who was made king over the realm of the Chaldeans— **2** in the first year of his reign, I, Daniel, perceived in the books the number of years that, according to the word of the LORD to Jeremiah the prophet, must pass before the end of the desolations of Jerusalem, namely, seventy years.

Daniel learns that the Lord has spoken to Jeremiah and declared desolations on his land for 70 years. This is found in both Jeremiah 25 and 29, but Daniel is likely reading the letter from Jeremiah to the captives in Babylon recorded in Jeremiah 29. Jeremiah tells the captives to settle in, build houses, and seek the good welfare of the city they are in. He follows, *"For thus says the Lord: After 70 years are completed at Babylon, I will visit you and perform My good word toward you, and cause you to return to this place."*

Daniel is reading this in the first year of King Darius which is likely a reference to Cyrus in 539 BC.[10] You can imagine Daniel getting excited since he was likely deported to Babylon in, or shortly after, 605 BC. Daniel is some 66 years into a 70-year exile. We know by the prayer that follows in verse 3 that

---

[10] Daniel 6:28 says, *"So this Daniel prospered in the reign of Darius and in the reign of Cyrus the Persian."* NKJV The Cultural Background Study Bible, Zondervan, 2017, pg. 1485, states, *"This can be translated, the reign of Darius, that is, the reign of Cyrus."*

Daniel understands scripture. He knows their return is not automatic; it depends on their repentance. Daniel seems familiar with Leviticus 26.

> Leviticus 26:40-42
>
> [40] "But if they confess their iniquity and the iniquity of their fathers in their treachery that they committed against me, and also in walking contrary to me, [41] so that I walked contrary to them and brought them into the land of their enemies—if then their uncircumcised heart is humbled and they make amends for their iniquity, [42] then I will remember my covenant with Jacob, and I will remember my covenant with Isaac and my covenant with Abraham, and I will remember the land.

Daniel 9:3-19 is a prayer of repentance and a plea for mercy. His prayer is full of references to "we" and "us" and even to the sins of their fathers. He understands the need for national repentance based on Leviticus 26. Daniel is favored in Heaven, so Gabriel is sent to acknowledge Daniel's prayer and to deliver both good and bad news. The good news is God has plans to finish transgression, to put an end to sin, to atone for iniquity, to bring in everlasting righteousness, and more (Daniel 9:24). The bad news is that it will take much longer than 70 years. There will be 70 sevens or 70 weeks of seven. Many scholars determine that to mean a period of 490 years. There will be 70 weeks of seven years.

> Daniel 9:24
>
> "Seventy weeks are decreed about your people and your holy city, to finish the transgression, to put an end to sin, and to atone for iniquity, to bring in everlasting righteousness, to seal both vision and prophet, and to anoint a most holy place.

Daniel does not record his response. He seems to say nothing. Why doesn't he argue with Gabriel? Why doesn't he demand that God keep his promise of 70 years? Because Daniel understands how God works and again relies on Leviticus 26. He understands the multiplication of seven. Daniel knows that God will judge his people for disobedience, and he understands the severity and length of God's discipline is based largely on their response to it. In Leviticus 26, God promises to bring four disastrous acts of judgment against Israel if they disobey his commands and go after other gods. He will bring upon them the sword, famine, pestilence, and wild beasts. If they fail to respond to his discipline, he says, *"...then I will discipline you again sevenfold for your sins..."* Four times in 11 verses, God promises to multiply their discipline seven times if they fail to repent. (Leviticus 26:18, 21, 24, 28) Daniel doesn't demand God keep his word because he understands that God is keeping his word. He is doing exactly what he promised to do. He is prolonging judgment because his people have not repented.

Seventy Weeks

This prophecy concerning 70 weeks is where the idea of a seven-year tribulation comes from. The prophecy has three parts. Seven weeks, 62 weeks, which together total 69 weeks, and then there is the final week equaling 70 weeks. The first two parts are described in verse 25.

> Daniel 9:25
>
> [25] Know therefore and understand that from the going out of the word to restore and build Jerusalem to the coming of an anointed one, a prince, there shall be seven weeks. Then for sixty-two weeks, it shall be built again with squares and moat, but in a troubled time.

The last part is in verse 27.

> Daniel 9:27
>
> [27] And he shall make a strong covenant with many for one week, and for half of the week, he shall put an end to sacrifice and offering. And on the wing of abominations shall come one who makes desolate, until the decreed end is poured out on the desolator."

Because of the multitude of conclusions and how scholars come to those conclusions, I will not discuss how most figure the first century and the death of Jesus fulfilled the first 69 weeks of Daniel's 70-week prophecy. Many scholars believe that the crucifixion happens at the end of, or just after, the first two parts of Daniel's prophecy. I bring it up not to explain it but because it is the source of the idea of a seven-year tribulation. Many believe we still have one week to fulfill in Daniel's prophecy, the 70th seven, and they call it the seven-year Tribulation. They teach that there has been a pause between weeks 69 and 70.

I have come to disagree with this, though I believed it and taught it that way in the past. I came to my current conclusion because of Leviticus 26 and a few other passages that I think explain seventy-sevens, including one that quotes Jesus.

Leviticus 26 puts the responsibility on the people of Israel. If they serve God, he will bless them, but if they disobey and go after other gods, he will punish them and continue to punish them until they repent. Sevenfold doesn't simply mean seven times, it means until. God will punish them until they repent. He must do it this way because he has made a covenant with them, and he will not break it.

Leviticus 26:44

> Yet for all that, when they are in the land of their enemies, I will not spurn them, neither will I abhor them so as to destroy them utterly and break my covenant with them, for I am the LORD their God.

This same principle is repeated in Isaiah 27:7-8

> ⁷ Has he struck them as he struck those who struck them? Or have they been slain as their slayers were slain?

The answer is no. God has not utterly destroyed them like he did Assyria and Babylon. Rather, *by exile,* he judges Israel.

> ⁸ Measure by measure, by exile you contended with them; he removed them with his fierce breath in the day of the east wind. And again, in Jeremiah

Jeremiah 30:11

> ...I will make a full end of all the nations among whom I scattered you, but of you, I will not make a full end. I will discipline you in just measure, and I will by no means leave you unpunished.

God does not utterly destroy Israel because he made a covenant with them. Rather, he judges them first by the four disastrous acts of judgment and then by exile if they fail to repent. He will continue to do so until they repent. This is the meaning of sevenfold and seventy-sevens. Seven was symbolic in ancient near eastern and Israelite culture and literature. It communicated a sense of "fullness" or "completeness" שֶׁבַע (šĕ·ḇă') "Seven" is spelled with the same consonants as the word שָׂבֵעַ (śā·ḇēaʿ) "complete/full".[11] A better way to consider it is to say "satisfied." The meaning of seven should be thought of like this: Until God is satisfied.

When we read things like, *"Then the LORD said to him, "Not so! If anyone kills Cain, vengeance shall be taken on him sevenfold."* (Genesis 4:15) and *"If Cain's revenge is sevenfold, then Lamech's is seventy-sevenfold."* (Genesis 4:24) we aren't being asked to do math, we are being told that it will be complete. God will be satisfied in the vengeance he takes. When we read the words of Jesus in Matthew 18, we get the idea.

> Matthew 18:21-22
>
> [21] Then Peter came up and said to him, "Lord, how often will my brother sin against me, and I forgive him? As many as seven times?" [22] Jesus said to him, "I do not say to you seven times, but seventy-seven times."

In recent scholarship, Jesus' words in Matthew 18:21-22 have been translated 77 times like the ESV rather than 70 times seven as in the NKJV. Either way, interpreters take

---

[11] Studies in Biblical and Semitic Symbolism, Farbridge, Maurice H. London, 1923 Pg. 136-137 (Available in the public domain)

Jesus to mean infinitely. How often will my brother sin against me, and I forgive him? As many as seven? Jesus answered, 70 times seven or as often as it takes. Taking this into Daniel 9, we can understand that God is not saying to Daniel "490 years are decreed upon your people," but rather, he is saying that desolation is decreed upon the land until I am satisfied. In other words, until they repent.

If you can accept what I have presented as a possibility, then you can accept the possibility that the seven-year tribulation is a misunderstanding. There hasn't been a pause between the 69th and 70th week. It is ongoing as God waits for his people to repent.

Let's change direction and tackle a passage that is connected at the hip to Daniel 9:27 and the idea of the tribulation. It is Jesus' reference to the abomination of desolation spoken of by the prophet Daniel in Matthew 24, Mark 13, and Luke 21.

The Abomination of Desolation

Growing up in church in the 1980s, I heard a lot about the abomination of desolation. We were told that a new temple would be built in Jerusalem and that a man called the Antichrist would set himself up in the temple as God. This false Christ sitting in the temple would be known as the abomination of desolation. This idea comes partly from Daniel 9:24-27, Daniel's vision of 70 weeks. In Verse 27, we read...

> Daniel 9:27
>
> ²⁷ And he shall make a strong covenant with many for one week, and for half of the week, he shall put an end to sacrifice and offering. And on the wing of abominations shall come one who makes desolate, until the decreed end is poured out on the desolator."

Historically, this verse is connected to Antiochus Epiphanes, who desecrated the temple by offering pigs to Zeus on the altar of the Lord (168-167 BC). You can read about it in the books of the Maccabees. However, Jesus connected the passage from Daniel to what is considered by many as end-time events he described in Matthew 24 and Mark 13.

> Matthew 24:27
>
> ¹⁵ "So when you see the abomination of desolation spoken of by the prophet Daniel, standing in the holy place...

> Mark 13:14
>
> ¹⁴ "But when you see the abomination of desolation standing where he ought not to be (let the reader

understand), then let those who are in Judea flee to the mountains.

Since some biblical scholars connect the passage in Daniel 9 to the events of the Antiochus Epiphanes, and those events predate Jesus, they look into the future for a similar event to fulfill Jesus' prophecy. Someone will desecrate the temple like Antiochus did. For that to happen, we need the temple to be rebuilt because Rome destroyed the temple in AD 70. In 1948, Israel was reestablished in the land of Israel as a sovereign nation, making the rebuilding of the temple a possibility, thereby making its desolation by the antichrist a very real possibility.

The basic story goes like this. The temple will be rebuilt. The surrounding nations will be in an uproar about it and threaten Israel's existence. A charismatic ruler will step in and make a seven-year peace treaty with Israel and the surrounding nations, bringing peace to the middle east and making himself a leading candidate to become the dominant world leader. But after three and half years he will break the peace treaty and set himself up as God in the temple and demand to be worshiped. Thus, he will be the abomination of desolation referred to by the prophet Daniel, just as Jesus told his disciples in the above-mentioned passages (Matthew 24 and Mark 13).

There is one problem with that interpretation, the historian Luke, a Gentile who wrote the Gospel of Luke and the book of Acts. In Luke, he too tells us the story of Jesus leaving Jerusalem and lamenting over her. He, too, tells us about the questions the disciples asked our Lord and records for us Jesus' answer but in doing so, he gives us a different perspective. This is found in Luke 21.

We'll get to it, but first I want to ensure you know Matthew 24, Mark 13, and Luke 21 all tell the same story. Jesus is preaching in the temple, and he has just finished up his scathing discourse against the leadership in Jerusalem (see Matthew 23). This is the passage where you hear Jesus say, "Woe to you scribes and Pharisees…" Matthew 23 is also where we get a passage that I believe is directly related to the return of Christ. In Verses 37-39, as Jesus is leaving the temple, he says:

> Matthew 23:37-39
>
> [37] "O Jerusalem, Jerusalem, the city that kills the prophets and stones those who are sent to it! How often would I have gathered your children together as a hen gathers her brood under her wings, and you were not willing! [38] See, your house is left to you desolate. [39] For I tell you, you will not see me again, until you say, 'Blessed is he who comes in the name of the Lord.'"

As Jesus and his disciples are leaving the city, the disciples begin to talk about the great temple. Jesus responds by telling them it will all come down (Matthew 24:1-2, Mark 13:1-2, Luke 21:5-6). This, of course, sparks some curiosity and, I am sure, some angst. As soon as they get the chance, they come to Jesus privately to ask Jesus about what he said.

In Matthew 24:3, we read, *"As he sat on the Mount of Olives, the disciples came to him privately, saying, "Tell us, when will these things be, and what will be the sign of your coming and of the end of the age?"*

In Mark 13:4 we read, *"Tell us, when will these things be, and what will be the sign when all these things are about to be accomplished?"*

Then, in Luke 21:7, we read, *"And they asked him, 'Teacher, when will these things be, and what will be the sign when these things are about to take place?'"*

Each of these three verses are in response to Jesus telling his disciples that the temple will be destroyed.

I think we can agree that these stories are one in the same, differing only in that they come from the different perspectives of Matthew, Mark, and Luke. Luke and Mark would have received the information second-hand as historians. Luke is a Gentile, and has a Greek perspective, while Matthew and Mark give us a Hebrew perspective.

The following shows how those perspectives differ concerning the abomination of desolation.

Hebrew Perspective:

Matthew 24:27

[15] "So when you see the abomination of desolation spoken of by the prophet Daniel, standing in the holy place...

Mark 13:14

[14] "But when you see the abomination of desolation standing where he ought not to be (let the reader understand), then let those who are in Judea flee to the mountains.

Greek Perspective:

Luke 21:20

[20] "But when you see Jerusalem surrounded by armies, then know that its desolation has come near...

I'm sure you can see the difference. Matthew talks about *"the abomination of desolation standing in the Holy place."* Mark tells us the abomination of desolation is *"standing where he ought not stand."* But Luke says, when we see *"armies surrounding Jerusalem."* Luke takes what some scholars believe to be a man, the antichrist, or the abomination of desolation, and turns it into armies. Furthermore, Luke takes the Holy Place, thought by some scholars to be the temple, and makes it Jerusalem.

The abomination of desolation is essentially Hebrew slang used in the Old Testament that refers to the destruction of Israel because of their abominations. This is what we find in scripture. The abomination isn't the desolation; it's the cause of the desolation.

Daniel 9:27.

> [27] And he shall make a strong covenant with many for one week, and for half of the week, he shall put an end to sacrifice and offering. And on the wing of abominations shall come one who makes desolate, until the decreed end is poured out on the desolator."

The desolation referred to comes on the wing of abomination. It is another way of saying it comes because of abominations, and that is exactly what is promised throughout the Old Testament. Because of space, I am only going to include a single reference that makes the point. I chose this one because it says it more than once and it is very clear.

Ezekiel 33:23-29

Six Rules to Understand the REVELATION .213

> [23] The word of the LORD came to me: [24] "Son of man, the inhabitants of these waste places in the land of Israel keep saying, 'Abraham was only one man, yet he got possession of the land; but we are many; the land is surely given us to possess.' [25] Therefore say to them, Thus says the Lord GOD: You eat flesh with the blood and lift up your eyes to your idols and shed blood; shall you then possess the land? [26] You rely on the sword, you commit abominations, and each of you defiles his neighbor's wife; shall you then possess the land? [27] Say this to them, : Thus says the Lord GOD: As I live, surely those who are in the waste places shall fall by the sword, and whoever is in the open field I will give to the beasts to be devoured, and those who are in strongholds and in caves shall die by pestilence. [28] And I will make the land a desolation and a waste, and her proud might shall come to an end, and the mountains of Israel shall be so desolate that none will pass through. [29] Then they will know that I am the LORD,, when I have made the land a desolation and a waste because of all their abominations that they have committed.

Clearly, the subject is the people of Israel (Verse 24). Clearly, they have committed abominations (Verse 26). Therefore, God promises desolation (Verse 28). And if that wasn't enough, God clearly states it all in Verse 29. *"Then they will know that I am the Lord, when I have made the land a desolation and a waste because of all their abominations that they have committed."*

To confirm the point I am making, I encourage you to read the following passages on your own. Leviticus 26, specifically Verses 27-35, Jeremiah 7:29-34 (LXX, The Greek version of the Old Testament), Jeremiah 22:1-6, 44:2-6, 44:20-23.

Hopefully you get the point that desolation comes because of abomination. When Jesus says, "the abomination of desolation spoken of by the prophet Daniel," he means the abomination (the sins) that brings destruction. The antichrist standing in the temple is not the abomination. The abomination, in my opinion, is the rejection of the Messiah, and it brings the destruction that Luke describes as armies surrounding Jerusalem. This is exactly how it is presented in the passages above from the Old Testament. God uses the nations to judge his people who have committed abominations. This is what happened in AD 70 when Rome surrounded Jerusalem, breached the walls, and destroyed the city and the temple, fulfilling the very thing Jesus prophesied would happen.

Let's look again at Daniel 9:27. You should recognize the one word of importance. This one word ties us to what went before.

Daniel 9:27

²⁷ And he shall make a strong covenant with many for one week, and for half of the week, he shall put an end to sacrifice and offering. And on the wing of abominations shall come one who makes desolate, until the decreed end is poured out on the desolator."

Seventy sevens isn't 490 years, it is "until."

Again, notice that the one who makes desolate comes on the wing of abominations. It's another way of saying that desolation comes because of abominations. The rejection of the Messiah is why the desolation has come. In 70 AD, Rome came to destroy the city and the sanctuary because Jerusalem rejected their Messiah, and it happened exactly how Luke described it. Armies surrounded Jerusalem and did exactly what Jesus said they would do, *"Not one stone will be left here upon another."* He was confident it would happen because he will be the one who brings it. He is the rider on the white horse of Revelation 6 who brought the four disastrous acts of judgment (Revelation 6:8). By destroying the temple, the first part of the 70th week was fulfilled. Sacrifices were ended when the temple was destroyed. (See Daniel 9:27)

However, the desolation will remain *"until the decreed end is poured out on the desolator."* Does that sound familiar? It's a bit muddled because tradition has taught us to look for a man we will call the antichrist, but it is not a man. The desolator is Death and Satan and all of God's spiritual enemies, the armies of the fallen elohim who have led men astray. The entire complex of the fallen elohim. The powers, thrones, dominions, and spirits who have stood against God and his plan for humanity. Here's what Paul says about them...

> 1 Corinthians 15:24-26
>
> **24** Then comes the end, when he delivers the kingdom to God the Father after destroying every rule and every authority and power. **25** For he must reign until he has put all his enemies under his feet. **26** The last enemy to be destroyed is death.

We live in the "until" of 1 Corinthians 15:25 and Daniel 9:27. We live in the time when the king of Heaven is putting down the desolator. Those who have fallen are thrown into the bottomless pit awaiting judgment (Jude 6, 2 Peter 2:4). The rest are in a fight for their lives, opposing God at every turn, buying a few more days, months, years, and even decades or centuries (Ephesians 6:10-12).

In Revelation 9, we see these fallen elohim, those in prison from Jude 6 and 2 Peter, released from their prison to gather their counterparts to Jerusalem for the final judgment. Their king is named destroyer or destruction (9:11). In

Revelation 11:7, the beast that rises from the bottomless pit attacks the city and kills the two witnesses, but destruction is poured out on him, and his armies and God's people are saved.

Forty-Two Months

Revelation Chapter 11 begins.

Revelation 11:1-3

11 Then I was given a measuring rod like a staff, and I was told, "Rise and measure the temple of God and the altar and those who worship there, ² but do not measure the court outside the temple; leave that out, for it is given over to the nations, and they will trample the holy city for forty-two months. ³ And I will grant authority to my two witnesses, and they will prophesy for 1,260 days, clothed in sackcloth."

The 42 months, or 1260 days is the "until" of Daniel 9:27. John is telling us that what we are reading is the last half of the last week. The "until" where God is judging the fallen elohim and all those who have chosen to worship them. "Until" is fulfilled when God is satisfied. Then comes the end.

I stated earlier the idea of a seven-year tribulation comes from the belief that the 70th week of Daniel's 70 weeks is yet to come. Something we are waiting on. I hope you see now that there is a viable alternative. I hope you see the first half of Daniel's 70th week is fulfilled. It was fulfilled when the sacrifices were put away when the temple was destroyed. The last half of the week is the "until" of 1 Corinthians 15:25 and Psalm 110:1, the period of time we now live in, a period that we can participate in. We can hasten the day according to Peter (2 Peter 2:11-12). It is the period of time where the gospel of Jesus is spreading, and the people of God (Israel) come to a place of repentance while God simultaneously deals with his unseen enemies.

Further Evidence

There are other clues that John is not writing about a specific period of tribulation or a seven-year tribulation that is still off in the future. These clues are in the first few chapters of the Revelation.

The first is found in Revelation 1:9.

Revelation 1:9

[9] I, John, your brother and partner in the tribulation and the kingdom and the patient endurance that are in Jesus, was on the island called Patmos on account of the word of God and the testimony of Jesus.

John calls himself a brother in tribulation, and as proof, he offers up his current place of residence. It is the beautiful isle of Patmos. Obviously, I am not being serious. Patmos was a prison colony where John had been sent because he was preaching the good news of a new king.

Our next bit of evidence comes from his letter to the church in Smyrna.

> Revelation 2:9-10
>
> [9] "'I know your tribulation and your poverty (but you are rich) and the slander of those who say that they are Jews and are not, but are a synagogue of Satan. [10] Do not fear what you are about to suffer. Behold, the devil is about to throw some of you into prison, that you may be tested, and for ten days, you will have tribulation. Be faithful unto death, and I will give you the crown of life.

Next is Revelation 2:13…

> Revelation 2:13
>
> [13] "'I know where you dwell, where Satan's throne is. Yet you hold fast my name, and you did not deny my faith even in the days of Antipas, my faithful witness, who was killed among you, where Satan dwells…'"

Hopefully you see where this is going. John didn't live in a time of peace; he and his fellow believers were experiencing the tribulation many today believe is still in the future.

Look at the letter to the church at Philadelphia.

Revelation 3:10-11

¹⁰ Because you have kept my word about patient endurance, I will keep you from the hour of trial that is coming on the whole world, to try those who dwell on the earth. ^{11.} I am coming soon. Hold fast to what you have, so that no one may seize your crown.

John is likely referring to the coming Christian persecution by the Romans under Nero. He is known for his cruel punishments and is often thought of as the original antichrist, with variations of his name equaling 666 using gematria. Many believe he will reincarnate to be the last-days antichrist. That is not the case.

John does not seem to have a future tribulation in mind. He isn't warning the seven churches to prepare for something they will never see. In some cases, they are experiencing tribulation, and in others, he tells them to expect it. It is easy to think of the tribulation as the future from our church pews in the cool of our air-conditioned buildings, but much of the world is experiencing tribulation and has been. The things Jesus talks about in Matthew 24, Mark 13, and Luke 21 aren't future; they began in the first century and are present and ongoing today. Israel was destroyed, the temple taken apart brick by brick. The Jews have experienced exile and periods of extreme persecution. Over six million of them were killed in the Holocaust. There have been other periods of extreme tribulation. The world wars, the Rwandan genocide. Most of the water in the world is undrinkable. Vast plots of land are uninhabitable. Famines, pestilence, and war persist all over the world. Wildfires, wild weather patterns, tremendous earthquakes are the norm, not the exception. Just because we are largely immune from it here in America isn't reason to doubt they exist. These things do exist in the world today. Our immunity isn't reason to ignore them. Rather, we should shine the light of the kingdom in them. I wonder what a difference would have been made if, during the holocaust, the church would have stood up to Hitler and shown the people of God, Israel, that their God cares about them.

The tribulation is current and happening all over the world. The king is going forth conquering and to conquer. His enemies are fighting for their lives, but still he prevails. He is shaking the nations; his people are returning to the land, and his witness to the world is going forth. The quicker we realize it and engage, the quicker his kingdom will come.

1000 years, Literal or Hyperbole?

The idea of a millennial reign comes from Revelation 20, where three times in 10 verses, John uses 1000 years to describe a period of time where Satan is imprisoned and the saints rule with Christ. So important is the millennial reign that many end-time systems are labeled based on what they believe about it. There is the premillennial camp that believes Christ returns before the millennial reign. There is the postmillennial camp that believes Christ returns after the millennial reign. Then there is the millennial camp, which doesn't believe in an earthly millennial reign at all. Among these groups and others there are varying meanings applied to John's words. These range from literal to metaphorical and anywhere in between.

That brings us to the question I hope to answer in the following paragraphs: What does John mean when he writes 1000 years?

Here are the three times John mentions 1000 years:

Revelation 20:2

[2] And he seized the dragon, that ancient serpent, who is the devil and Satan, and bound him for a thousand years.

Revelation 20:4

...They came to life and reigned with Christ for a thousand years.

Revelation 20:7

And when the thousand years are ended, Satan will be released from his prison.

These verses are widely accepted as literal. These are the premillennialists and the dispensationalists. Those who hold to this idea believe John writes and means there will be a literal 1000-year imprisonment for Satan and earthly millennial reign for Christ. He will rule from his throne in Israel, after which Satan will be released from his prison for one last rebellion. But there are other ideas about John's meaning. I will express some of those ideas below and sprinkle my own thoughts throughout.

In The Jewish Annotated New Testament, the word "thousand" is said to signify "a sufficient enormity." (Article: Page 550, The Numerology of Revelation) I believe this definition helps us understand Revelation 7 and John's description of the 12,000 Jews from each of the 12 tribes. I doubt we should think that only 12,000 from each tribe will be sealed or that only 144,000 Jews in total will be sealed. The number represents something much larger. Somewhere between John's 144,000 and Paul's "all Israel will be saved" from Romans 11:26.

The note on Revelation 20:2 in the Passion Translation presents the 1000 years as a metaphor similar to the Jewish Annotated New Testament.

Satan has been bound since the death and resurrection of Jesus. We now enforce the judgment that took place on Calvary. The thousand years is an obvious metaphor for the time in which we live (2 Peter 3:8). We are given the authority to "overpower the mighty man and tie him up" and plunder his goods (Mark 3:27). See also Matthew 12:29; John 12:31; Colossians 2:15.[12]

How many of you believe Brain Simmons, editor of the TPT, has lost his mind?

Well, if you do, I should proceed carefully because I agree, but describe it as John using hyperbole rather than metaphor. Hyperbole is an exaggerated statement or claim not meant to be taken literally. John simply means a long time. We find hyperbole tied to 1000 in other places in scripture. So, we can apply one of our keys here. John is familiar with his Old Testament, and he uses it to help us understand what he is seeing.

---

[12] Brian Simmons, trans., *The Passion Translation* (BroadStreet Publishing, 2017).

1000 as figurative (hyperbole) in the Old Testament

- Deuteronomy 1:10-11, 32:30
- Joshua 23:10
- Job 9:3, 33:23
- Psalm 50:10, 84:10, 90:4, 91:7,
- Ecclesiastes 6:6, 7:28
- Song of Solomon 4:4
- Isaiah 7:23, 30:17
- Daniel 7:10
- Amos 5:3

Especially:

Deuteronomy 7:9

Know therefore that the Lord your God is God, the faithful God who keeps covenant and steadfast love with those who love him and keep his commandments, to a thousand generations…

1 Chronicles 16:14-18

[14] He is the Lord our God; his judgments are in all the earth.

¹⁵ Remember his covenant forever, the word that he commanded, for a thousand generations,

¹⁶ the covenant that he made with Abraham, his sworn promise to Isaac,

¹⁷ which he confirmed to Jacob as a statute, to Israel as an everlasting covenant,

¹⁸ saying, "To you, I will give the land of Canaan, as your portion for an inheritance."

Psalm 105:7-11

⁷ He is the Lord our God; his judgments are in all the earth.

⁸ He remembers his covenant forever, the word that he commanded, for a thousand generations,

⁹ the covenant that he made with Abraham, his sworn promise to Isaac,

¹⁰, which he confirmed to Jacob as a statute, to Israel as an everlasting covenant,

¹¹ saying, "To you I will give the land of Canaan as your portion for an inheritance."

In these three passages that are practically identical, should we ask if the covenant is only to 1000 generations? I think not. Rather, we are to know that "a thousand generations" refers to an incalculable eternity. It means forever so long as the conditions are met.

Steve Gregg, in his book *Revelation, Four Views*, says, "The number 'a thousand' is frequently used in scripture without the intention of conveying statistical information."

Furthermore, the expression "a thousand years" is never used elsewhere in scripture for an actual number of years, but only to suggest the idea of a very long time. (Psalm 90:4, Ecclesiastes 6:6, 2 Peter 3:8)[13]

> Psalm 90:4, for example:
>
> [4] For a thousand years in your sight are but as yesterday when it is past, or as a watch in the night.
>
> And Ecclesiastes 6:6…
>
> [6] Even though he should live a thousand years twice over, yet enjoy no good—do not all go to the one place?

As stated previously, I believe John is using hyperbole. The 1000-year reign described in Revelation 20 does not have a prescribed start and ending date like a lease or a business contract. It describes a long time. It describes a sufficient enormity as quoted above from the Jewish Annotated New Testament. We have examples from the book of Enoch

---

[13] Revelation Four Views, Gregg, Steve, Thomas Nelson Publishers, 1997.

concerning similar situations to Satan's imprisonment that do the same thing.

Speaking of Azazel, one of the fallen watchers, Enoch uses hyperbole to describe the length of his imprisonment on death row, so to speak:

> In Enoch 10:4-6, we read:
>
> > [4] And again the Lord said to Raphael: 'Bind Azâzêl hand and foot and cast him into the darkness: and make an opening in the desert, which is in Dûdâêl, and cast him therein. [5] And place upon him rough and jagged rocks, and cover him with darkness, and let him abide there forever, and cover his face that he may not see the light. [6] And on the day of the great judgment, he shall be cast into the fire.[14]

Here, Enoch tells us that Azazel will be bound forever (Verse 5), but in the very next verse, we are told he is taken from that place and cast into fire on the day of great judgment. The first place can't be Azazel's eternal punishment (forever) if he is taken from it and cast into fire. The author is using hyperbole.

Also, in Enoch 10, this time Verses 11-13 we read:

---

[14] R. H. Charles and W. O. E. Oesterley, *The Book of Enoch* (London: Society for Promoting Christian Knowledge, 1917), Enoch 10:4–6.

¹¹ And the Lord said unto Michael: 'Go, **bind** Semjâzâ and his associates who have united themselves with women so as to have defiled themselves with them in all their uncleanness. ¹² And, when their sons have slain one another, and they have seen the destruction of their beloved ones, bind them fast for seventy generations in the **valleys** of the earth, till the day of their judgment and of their consummation, till the judgment that is forever and ever is consummated. ¹³ In those days they shall be led off to the abyss of fire: áandñ to the torment and the prison in which they shall be confined for ever.[15]

In this passage, "70 generations" is used in place of "forever" in Verse 4-6.

Dr. Heiser notes in his Companion to the Book of Enoch, *"seventy generations – The description here of the duration of the Watchers' punishment differs from the "forever" of Verses 4 and 5. The difference is superficial, as "seventy generations" reflects a numerical typology that refers to "the rest of time" (the end of history)."*

In another passage from Enoch, the hyperbole is clear.

Enoch 18:16

---

[15] R. H. Charles and W. O. E. Oesterley, *The Book of Enoch* (London: Society for Promoting Christian Knowledge, 1917), Enoch 10:11–13.

¹⁶ And He was wroth with them, and bound them till the time when their guilt should be consummated (even) for ten thousand years.'[16]

"Til the time..." in the first part of the verse turns into "even 10,000 years" in the second part. It is clear hyperbole, and it is a similar situation to what we read in Revelation 20:1-3 and Revelation 20:7-10. It is a length of time set aside to accomplish something. Satan is locked up until the time comes to judge Gog and Magog, like the fallen elohim (the host of heaven, the stars as they are called in Enoch 18) is imprisoned until the time of their guilt comes to completion. It ends in eternal flames.

Of Enoch 18:16, Michael Heiser writes, *"ten thousand years – More literally, 'a myriad of years' (compare 21:6). Consequently, the point is not a countable number."* (Companion to the Book of Enoch)

Enoch continues the hyperbole in 21:6.

⁶ These are of the number of the stars of heaven which have transgressed the commandment of the Lord, and are bound here till ten thousand years, the time entailed by their sins, are consummated.'[17]

---

[16] R. H. Charles and W. O. E. Oesterley, *The Book of Enoch* (London: Society for Promoting Christian Knowledge, 1917), Enoch 18:16.
[17] R. H. Charles and W. O. E. Oesterley, *The Book of Enoch* (London: Society for Promoting Christian Knowledge, 1917), Enoch 21:6.

About this passage, Dr. Heiser writes, "*The time entailed by their sins* – Ethiopis reads 'the number' of their sins. The wording is interesting, for it suggests that, just as the time of the imprisonment ('myriad of years'– i.e., an uncountable number) is beyond numbering, so is the extent of the Watchers; sins (i.e., that its magnitude cannot be calculated)."[18]

In laymen's terms, it is hyperbole. Every time reference in these passages is an example of hyperbole. They are speaking of fallen Elohim being arrested and held until the time when their guilt should be consummated. "Consummated" means to complete or make perfect. Effectively, these fallen Elohim are on death row, waiting for execution for their sins. Satan included. 1000 years, 10,000 years, and 70 generations are all examples of hyperbole telling us that it will be a long time coming. Even the end of time.

Open Ended

Describing the same event or types of events (the imprisoning of the fallen Elohim), both Jude and Peter forego hyperbole, using clearer language.

---

[18] M. S. Heiser A Companion to the Book of Enoch (Crane, MO: Defender, 2019)

Jude 6

⁶ And the angels who did not stay within their own position of authority, but left their proper dwelling, he has kept in eternal chains under gloomy darkness until the judgment of the great day—

2 Peter 2:4

⁴ For if God did not spare angels when they sinned, but cast them into hell and committed them to chains of gloomy darkness to be kept until the judgment…

When saying the fallen angels are held in chains "until," Jude and Peter are clearly speaking of the same events referenced by Enoch – as well as John's imprisonment of Satan. There's a comparison in Enoch 18:16. I mentioned it earlier, "til the time, even 10,000 years." Isaiah's apocalypse conveys the same thing about the same event: the imprisonment of the host of heaven.

Isaiah 24:21-23

²¹ On that day, the Lord will punish the host of heaven, in heaven, and the kings of the earth, on the earth.

²² They will be gathered together as prisoners in a pit; they will be shut up in a prison, and after many days, they will be punished.

> ²³ Then the moon will be confounded and the sun ashamed, for the Lord of hosts reigns on Mount Zion and in Jerusalem, and his glory will be before his elders.

The host of heaven, clearly the sun, moon, and stars, from Deuteronomy that God has given to the nations to worship, are judged (see Psalm 82), and are held in prison for many days. Like Jude and Peter, the author here foregoes hyperbole and goes with "many days." "Many days" is synonymous with "until" from Jude 6 and 2 Peter 2:4, and I believe synonymous with Enoch's and John's use of hyperbole, 1000 years, 10,000 years, 70 generations, and forever.

Joseph Blenkinshopp writes about Isaiah 24:22, "The theme of the binding of these malevolent celestial powers, with whom the rulers of the nations are—in the apocalyptic world view—in league, is also well attested in apocalyptic writings (e.g. Enoch 18:11–19:3; 90:24–25; Jude 13; 2 Peter 2:4). **The author of the Christian apocalypse, the book of Revelation, follows the Isaian text in presenting the hostile powers under their king, the angel Abaddon, imprisoned in a dark and bottomless pit (Revelation 9:2, 11). There will be a lapse of time, estimated by the same apocalyptic writer as 1,000 years (Revelation 20:1–3 cf. Enoch 91:12–17), between their imprisonment and the**

execution of the sentence. This interval allows for different baroque elaborations in apocalyptic circles and continues to provide an occasion for speculation among readers of apocalyptic sentiment today. It ends, as our passage makes clear, with the establishment and universal acknowledgment of the rule of God throughout the cosmos." (Bold type added)

What I am labeling hyperbole Blenkinshopp calls estimation. I think it is clear that the hyperbole of Revelation 20 refers to the time it takes to accomplish all God wants to accomplish. It is not a set time because God has not decreed a time. Rather, he is patient toward us. As explained in Romans 2:4, and 2 Peter 3:8-10, God wants all to come to repentance.

It is clear from other passages that there is a passing of time where things are taking place to which God does not ascribe a length of time.

> I Corinthians 15:25-26
>
> [25] For he must reign until he has put all his enemies under his feet. [26] The last enemy to be destroyed is death.[1]
>
> Psalm 110:1
>
> [1] The Lord says to my Lord: "Sit at my right hand until I make your enemies your footstool."

Romons 11:25-26

25 Lest you be wise in your own sight, I do not want you to be unaware of this mystery, brothers: a partial hardening has come upon Israel until the fullness of the Gentiles has come in. **26** And in this way all Israel will be saved, as it is written,

"The Deliverer will come from Zion. He will banish ungodliness from Jacob…"

Like Jude and Peter, both Paul and the Psalmist simply say "until" to describe a period of time that passes to accomplish the same thing. There is a period of time that passes in which Gentiles come to repentance, Israel accepts their Messiah, and Jesus puts his enemies under his feet. This period of time is still ongoing today. As I've stated elsewhere, "We live in the until." I could add to that now that we live in the 1000 years of Revelation 20. (That might have been clear in our study of recapitulation, where I stated that Revelation 20 is the story of Christ from start to finish.)

I believe we have a hard time accepting John's use of hyperbole because we have a wrong view of inspiration. We have a hard time accepting that inspiration allows for hyperbole or exaggerated speech. If God inspired scripture, then surely John means exactly 1000 years when he writes 1000 years. This concept of Inspiration allows us to dismiss the use of hyperbole in Enoch because most will not accept Enoch as inspired. I don't need Enoch to be inspired to accept that John, like Enoch, uses hyperbole. It is an accepted form of communication in the culture. They use hyperbole, idioms, typology, and metaphor. Things are not always exact even when they are presented as such, like Revelation 7. Few believe only 3000 people were saved on the Day of Pentecost. Few believe it was only 5000 people who were fed by the loaves and fishes. It is widely accepted that the numbers are an estimation of the men, while the women and children were not counted at all. In fact, the authors use "about" when giving us those numbers, yet with a strict definition of inspiration, we could ask, why doesn't God tell us exactly? The author tells us exactly how many fish are caught when Jesus feeds the disciples after his resurrection: 153 fish.

Rather, we should allow for the biblical authors to be human. They are not robots, and they are not in trances as they write. God chose them because of who they were, where they were, and when they were in history. They speak in accord with their culture and their personalities, and their experiences shine through in their writings. God doesn't need to sedate them or magically possess them to get the desired message across. He doesn't freak out when they use an idiom or hyperbole to convey their thoughts. When Peter is quoting Psalm 90:4 (2 Peter 3:8), he isn't giving us a math formula like

1000 years = 1 day. He is simply saying that 1000 years isn't a long time to the Lord. It's as short as one day. In fact, the Psalmist says, "or a watch in the night." Is Peter editing the psalmist? Did the psalmist get it incorrect, and Peter felt the need to correct him by removing that part? Or is it possible that they are both conveying the same idea, that is, God isn't bound by our calendars or our ideas about time? What is a long time to us is really nothing to him.

Enoch and John are using hyperbole to communicate to us the fallen Elohim will be imprisoned for a long time, waiting for their final judgment. Isaiah does the same with "many days," and Jude and Peter simply say, "until." The 1000-year period of Revelation 20 is hyperbole, and it marks a time that is ongoing.

Daniel 7 And Satan's Death

In Daniel 7, Daniel records for us the "visions of his head as he lay in his bed." Simply put, he writes down a dream. He tells us about four separate beasts who are called up from the great sea by the four winds of heaven. They are described as follows:

Daniel 7:4-7

> [4] The first was like a lion and had eagles' wings. Then as I looked, its wings were plucked off, and it was lifted up from the ground and made to stand on two feet like a man, and the mind of a man was given to it.

> [5] And behold, another beast, a second one, like a bear. It was raised up on one side. It had three ribs in its mouth between its teeth; and it was told, 'Arise, devour much flesh.'

> [6] After this, I looked, and behold, another, like a leopard, with four wings of a bird on its back. And the beast had four heads, and dominion was given to it.

> [7] After this, I saw in the night visions, and behold, a fourth beast, terrifying and dreadful and exceedingly strong. It had great iron teeth; it devoured and broke in pieces and stamped what was left with its feet. It was

different from all the beasts that were before it, and it had ten horns.

The fourth beast has 10 horns, and we are told that a mouth was given to one of the horns and it was saying great things.

When the four beasts are considered together, they have seven heads and 10 horns because the third beast has four heads, and the fourth beast has 10 horns. Horns are signs of authority in the Bible. Considering them together becomes important when we come to John's Revelation.

In the book of Revelation, we are told John is on the isle of Patmos for the word of the Lord and that he is in the spirit on the Lord's Day. He is invited into Heaven (4:1) and shown many things. Like John, he has a heavenly perspective. In chapter 12, he introduces a dragon with seven heads and 10 horns. On each of his heads, there is a crown (Revelation 12:3). Chapter 12 ends, and 13 begins with the introduction of a second dragon. He, too, has seven heads and 10 horns. This one is called a beast.

Here's the relevant passage without the chapter break and verse numbers:

Revelation 12:17 - Revelation 13:4

Then the dragon became furious with the woman and went off to make war on the rest of her offspring, on those who keep the commandments of God and hold to the testimony of Jesus. And he stood on the sand of the sea. And I saw a beast rising out of the sea, with ten horns and seven heads, with ten diadems on its horns and blasphemous names on its heads. And the beast that I saw was like a leopard; its feet were like a bear's, and its mouth was like a lion's mouth. And to it, the dragon gave his power and his throne and great authority. One of its heads seemed to have a mortal wound, but its mortal wound was healed, and the whole earth marveled as they followed the beast. And they worshiped the dragon, for he had given his authority to the beast, and they worshiped the beast, saying, "Who is like the beast, and who can fight against it?"

The similarities to Daniel 7 are easy enough to see. The four beasts from Daniel 7 are combined into a single beast in Revelation 13. There are seven heads, 10 horns, and it is described as having characteristics of a leopard, a bear, and a lion like the first three beasts from Daniel 7. Furthermore, it has blasphemous names on it, like the great words spoken by the fourth beast of Daniel 7. Despite being combined into one beast, there is a difference in the two passages I've presented. In Revelation 13, one of the seven heads seems to have a mortal wound, but its mortal wound is healed.

Daniel doesn't miss this detail. He accounts for it a few verses later. In Daniel's dream, thrones appear, and the Ancient of Days takes center stage. Before him stood "*ten thousand times ten thousand*" to witness what was about to take place. It is an obvious courtroom scene. God and his counsel have come to judge the beasts. Verses 11-12 tell of the verdict.

> 11 "I looked then because of the sound of the great words that the horn was speaking. And as I looked, the beast was killed, and its body destroyed and given over to be burned with fire. 12 As for the rest of the beasts, their dominion was taken away, but their lives were prolonged for a season and a time.

The fourth beast of Daniel 7, who accounts for one head, is killed and is burned with fire. This aligns nicely with the details of John's vision in Revelation 13, where one head is mortally wounded.

The only notable difference is the wounded head of Revelation 13 is resurrected. Daniel does not account for that detail in his dream, though he may later in chapter 9.

The Four Beasts

Daniel was perplexed by what he saw, and he wanted an explanation. He approached one of those who stood there, presumably one of the many millions introduced in Verse 10 and asked him what the meaning of it was. Specifically, he wants to know about the fourth beast who is more terrible than the others.

He answers Daniel by explaining the four beasts are four kings who shall arise out of the earth. Here is where I part from more traditional views. Generally, these four beasts are connected to Babylon, Persia, Greece, and Rome. Rome is the fourth beast. From there, and quite naturally, the kingdoms are aligned with their most famous kings, Nebuchadnezzar, Cyrus, Alexander the Great, and Nero. Nero fits the description of the horn who speaks great things against God's people because of his merciless persecution of the early church. There is some truth in all of this; it fits and cannot be ignored. However, what happens in doing this kind of alignment with the historical facts is that we miss the real story. We miss the unseen supernatural side that is the foundation of it all. We miss that the Ancient of Days is judging the fallen elohim.

This is nowhere more apparent than in Daniel 10, where we are introduced to the Prince of Persia, and the Prince of Greece. The Prince of Persia battles the angels from God, clearly marking them as something other than earthly princes. These are the powers and spiritual forces in heavenly places spoken of by Paul in the New Testament. These fallen elohim cannot be ignored if we hope to understand what is happening in Daniel 7 and in Revelation 12. The beast in Revelation 13 isn't a man called the antichrist, it is the alliance of these spiritual forces who are empowered to rule by the dragon in Revelation 13. They are the spirit of the antichrist.

The Resurrected Beast

Like I said earlier, Daniel doesn't explicitly state that the fourth beast is resurrected. I believe it is implied, but that's a discussion for another time. John, however, does introduce a resurrected beast. His first introduction comes in the first Act of Revelation 4-11. In Revelation 9, an army of locusts, whom I believe to be the fallen angels of Jude 6 and 2 Peter 2:4, are released from the bottomless pit. In 9:11, we are introduced to their king. His name is Abaddon in Hebrew and Apollyon in Greek. In English, we can call him the Destroyer. We see the Destroyer again in Chapter 11 where he has gathered *some from the peoples and tribes and languages and nations.* There he is called, "the beast that rises from the bottomless pit" (11:7) and he has gathered his army against Jerusalem and the two witnesses who represent the people of God (Israel). Those witnesses are Judah and Joseph and the people associated with each (Ezekiel 37).

The second introduction comes in Act 3, Revelation 17-19. In Act 3, we have a beast similar to the one in Revelation 13, but it is similar to that of Revelation 12 too. I believe the description in Revelation 17 is ambiguous on purpose.

> Revelation 17:1-3
>
> **17** Then one of the seven angels who had the seven bowls came and said to me, "Come, I will show you the judgment of the great prostitute who is seated on many waters, **2** with whom the kings of the earth have committed sexual immorality, and with the wine of whose sexual immorality the dwellers on earth have become drunk." **3** And he carried me away in the Spirit into a wilderness, and I saw a woman sitting on a scarlet beast that was full of blasphemous names, and it had seven heads and ten horns.

This beast is red, has seven heads and 10 horns. Unlike in Revelation 12 and 13, this beast has no crowns. Crowns are one of the ways we can distinguish the dragon from the beast. In Revelation 12 the dragon has crowns on his heads while the beast in Revelation 13 wears his crowns on his horns. Another ambiguous description is the color of the beast and that he seems to have blasphemous names tattooed on him. The dragon of Revelation 12 is red, but the beast of Chapter 13 has a mouth speaking blasphemous things. We might then see that being full of blasphemous names is less about tattoos and more about being full of something that comes out of the mouth. It manifests in words.

With what we have so far, it is impossible to tell who the beast of Revelation 17 is. Is he the dragon? Or is he the beast? The answer might be Yes to both!

I believe John is purposefully ambiguous because we aren't supposed to separate the two creatures as if they are something altogether different. They really aren't. Look at what John says later in the chapter.

> Revelation 17:8
>
> The beast that you saw was and is not, and is about to rise from the bottomless pit and go to destruction. And the dwellers on earth whose names have not been written in the book of life from the foundation of the world will marvel to see the beast, because it was and is not and is to come.

John introduced the beast that rises from the bottomless pit in Revelation 9 and 11. He is Abaddon, Destroyer, who has come against Jerusalem to kill the two witnesses. But he does one better than that in Act 4. In Revelation 20, he identifies the beast that rises from the bottomless pit as Satan.

> Revelation 20:1-3

20 Then I saw an angel coming down from heaven, holding in his hand the key to the bottomless pit and a great chain. ² And he seized the dragon, that ancient serpent, who is the devil and Satan, and bound him for a thousand years, ³ and threw him into the pit, and shut it and sealed it over him, so that he might not deceive the nations any longer, until the thousand years were ended. After that, he must be released for a little while.

Revelation 20:7-9

⁷ And when the thousand years are ended, Satan will be released from his prison ⁸ and will come out to deceive the nations that are at the four corners of the earth, Gog and Magog, to gather them for battle; their number is like the sand of the sea. ⁹ And they marched up over the broad plain of the earth and surrounded the camp of the saints and the beloved city, but fire came down from heaven and consumed them...

Satan is bound and thrown into the bottomless pit and kept until he is resurrected for the purpose of gathering the nations from the four corners to Jerusalem. You'll remember that this is exactly what the beast who rises from the bottomless pit does in Act 1. He gathers an army of 200 million to the city where the Lord was crucified and kills the two witnesses who represent all of Israel. This army is described as *"some from the peoples and tribes and languages and nations."* That's another way of saying people from the four corners of the earth, like Revelation 20:7-9.

Therefore, we can deduce that the beast of Chapter 17, who *"is about to rise from the bottomless pit,"* is the dragon of Revelation 12 and 20, which is Satan, who also rises from the bottomless pit.

Revelation 12:9

⁹ And the great dragon was thrown down, that ancient serpent, who is called the devil and Satan, the deceiver of the whole world...

Revelation 20:2-3a

² And he seized the dragon, that ancient serpent, who is the devil and Satan, and bound him for a thousand years, ³ and threw him into the pit...

Seems logical to me. The pieces fit together. But I believe we have gotten ahead of ourselves. As I said before, the ambiguity is on purpose. I don't believe we are supposed to separate the dragon and the beast. They are so closely linked together that they are as one. Let's return to Act 3 and cChapter 17 to explain what I mean.

Revelation 17:11

¹¹ As for the beast that was and is not, it is an eighth, but it belongs to the seven, and it goes to destruction.

The beast that was and is not, is separate but also part of the seven. The seventh is the eighth. How so? Because the seventh head is mortally wounded but is resurrected. It was and is not and will rise from the bottomless pit (it will be resurrected).

The elohim named in the Revelation who comes from the bottomless pit is Satan. John tells us this plainly in Revelation 20:1-3 and verse 7. Satan is the mortally wounded head of the beast in chapter 13. He is Abaddon who rises from the pit in Chapter 9 and 11, and he is the fourth beast that is killed in Daniel 7. What does it mean for an elohim to be killed? What are we supposed to know about that?

Just briefly, we need to know that the bottomless pit is synonymous with everything we associate with the grave. To be killed, as the fourth beast was in Daniel 7, is to be sent into the underworld, into Sheol or the grave. Satan is thrown into the pit in Revelation 20. The Greek word is ἄβυσσος (abyssos), the abyss. For the sake of space, I won't add it here, but you might remember that legion, the group of demons who possessed the man in the wilderness, begged to not be cast into the abyss. They begged not to be sent into torment into the bottomless pit. These things are synonymous.

When in Daniel, we read the fourth beast was killed and burned with fire, it is synonymous with being told he is bound with chains to be tormented in the fires of the bottomless pit. He is being cast into Hell. Enoch describes it for us in Enoch 21. The abyss is a place without bottom or top burning with fire.

Back to the purposeful ambiguity. John doesn't want us to see the dragon and the beast as separate because the dragon has empowered the beast. He has brought the remaining elohim together to continue the work because he knows his time is short.

Revelation 12 describes the battle that takes place between Michael and his armies and Satan and his armies. This battle takes place during the life of Christ. Satan is defeated and cast out of heaven, where he turns his fury on the woman who has given birth to Jesus. She represents Israel. We are told, *"...woe to you, O earth and sea, for the devil has come down to you in great wrath, because he knows that his time is short!"* (Revelation 12:12).

Knowing his time is short, he pursues the woman, and he makes plans. We quoted this passage earlier, but now it is time to shed light on what it really tells us.

Revelation 12:17-Revelation 13:4

Then the dragon became furious with the woman and went off to make war on the rest of her offspring, on those who keep the commandments of God and hold to the testimony of Jesus. And he stood on the sand of the sea. And I saw a beast rising out of the sea, with ten horns and seven heads, with ten diadems on its horns and blasphemous names on its heads. And the beast that I saw was like a leopard; its feet were like a bear's, and its mouth was like a lion's mouth. And to it, the dragon gave his power and his throne and great authority. One of its heads seemed to have a mortal wound, but its mortal wound was healed, and the whole earth marveled as they followed the beast. And they worshiped the dragon, for he had given his authority to the beast, and they worshiped the beast, saying, "Who is like the beast, and who can fight against it?"

Knowing his time is short, and that soon he will be thrown into the bottomless pit, his prison, Satan calls for the former world leaders to gather and align with him against the God of Heaven and his newly appointed king, Yeshua, Jesus the Messiah.

These fallen elohim are the three beasts who were spared in Daniel 7, which is why the single beast in Revelation 13 looks exactly like them. They are empowered by Satan, who is the fourth and most terrible beast in Daniel 7, which is why John tells us in Revelation 17 that the seventh head that is killed is resurrected and becomes part of the seven again as an eighth. Revelation 20 tells us he is resurrected to gather the nations for judgment. This is expressed in Revelation 11 and 16. You might remember that in Chapter 16, spirits like frogs come from the mouths of Satan, the beast, and the false prophets to deceive the kings of the earth and gather them for battle.

This idea that Satan is bound and others do his work is expressed in other New Testament passages.

In Ephesians 6, we are told to put on the whole armor of God to protect ourselves from the schemes of the devil, and then we are told, *"For we do not wrestle against flesh and blood, but against the rulers, against the authorities, against the cosmic powers over this present darkness, against the spiritual forces of evil in the heavenly places."* Who do we wrestle against? Not Satan, but the powers and authorities over this present age. These are those who were empowered in Revelation 13:1-4.

In Ephesians 2, Paul calls it the course of this world, the prince of the power of the air, the spirit that is now at work in the sons of disobedience. This is the spirit of the antichrist that John tells us is already present in 1 John 4, just as Paul does in Ephesians 2.

You see, after the cross and resurrection, the powers who used to be enemies, remember the opposing princes from Daniel 10, are united. They have formed an alliance. This is why John can say there are many antichrists in chapter 2 and say there is a spirit of the antichrist in chapter 4.

The following is one of my favorite passages that helps explain what I am saying...

2 Thessalonians 2:7-12

> [7] For the mystery of lawlessness is already at work. Only he who now restrains it will do so until he is out of the way. [8] And then the lawless one will be revealed, whom the Lord Jesus will kill with the breath of his mouth and bring to nothing by the appearance of his coming. [9] The coming of the lawless one is by the activity of Satan with all power and false signs and wonders, [10] and with all wicked deception for those who are perishing, because they refused to love the truth and so be saved. [11] Therefore, God sends them a strong delusion, so that they may believe what is false, [12] in order that all may be condemned who did not believe the truth but had pleasure in unrighteousness.

There is one who is in the way of the coming of the lawless one, the one who restrains. In Revelation 9, there is an angel who has the key to the bottomless pit. In Revelation

20, an angel binds Satan with chains and throws him into the bottomless pit. Then, in Verse 7, Satan is released. One day this angel will be told to release the dragon. When that happens, the full power of the lawless one will be released onto the earth to deceive the nations into coming to their judgment. The coming of the lawless one is by the activity of Satan, who is released from the pit to gather Gog of Magog, the nations from the four corners to Jerusalem where God will deal, for the last time, with all the fallen elohim and those who follow them.

If Daniel 7 presents us with an order of events, and I believe it does, then we can conclude that Satan, the 4th beast of Daniel 7, was dealt with just prior to or at the ascension of the Son of Man, who is Jesus. The fourth beast is killed in Verses 11-12, and the son of man comes victoriously on the clouds in Verses 13-14. The one who spoke lies against the sinless son of man is found guilty of killing a sinless man, something he had no authority to do. The wages of sin is death, and Jesus had no sin by which he could be found worthy of death.

Jesus verifies this timeline for us.

> John 12:31
>
> "Now is the judgment of this world; now will the ruler of this world be cast out."

I doubt this needs to be done, but I will do it anyway. The Greek word for "now", is νῦν (*nyn*), and it is defined as ***just now***, *presently, a short while before, i.e., a time just before or after the discourse (Jn 11:8).*[19] John 12:31 comes just prior to the crucifixion, something Paul tells us the powers regret. 1 Corinthians 2:8 says, *"None of the rulers of this age understood this, for if they had, they would not have crucified the Lord of glory."* What could they have known that would have prevented them from killing Christ? That crucifying the Lord of glory signed their death warrants.

Speaking of the coming Holy Spirit, Jesus says this in John 16:

[8] And when he comes, he will convict the world concerning sin and righteousness and judgment: [9] concerning sin, because they do not believe in me; [10] concerning righteousness, because I go to the Father, and you will see me no longer; [11] concerning judgment, because the ruler of this world is judged. (John 16:8-11)

And then there is this story from Matthew 12.

Matthew 12:22-29

---

[19] James Swanson, *Dictionary of Biblical Languages with Semantic Domains: Greek (New Testament)* (Oak Harbor: Logos Research Systems, Inc., 1997).

22 Then a demon-oppressed man who was blind and mute was brought to him, and he healed him, so that the man spoke and saw. **23** And all the people were amazed, and said, "Can this be the Son of David?" **24** But when the Pharisees heard it, they said, "It is only by Beelzebul, the prince of demons, that this man casts out demons." **25** Knowing their thoughts, he said to them, "Every kingdom divided against itself is laid waste, and no city or house divided against itself will stand. **26** And if Satan casts out Satan, he is divided against himself. How, then, will his kingdom stand? **27** And if I cast out demons by Beelzebul, by whom do your sons cast them out? Therefore, they will be your judges. **28** But if it is by the Spirit of God that I cast out demons, then the kingdom of God has come upon you. **29** Or how can someone enter a strong man's house and plunder his goods, unless he first binds the strong man? Then, indeed, he may plunder his house.

While it may not be implicit, Jesus is telling us that Beelzebub, another name for Satan, is already bound, and Jesus is freely plundering his house by casting out demons. He is telling us that a new kingdom has come to them. It is the kingdom of God, and Jesus is its king.

Satan is imprisoned. He is the strong man who has been bound, Matthew 12. He is Abaddon who is locked behind the door of the bottomless pit (Revelation 9). He has been bound in chains in the abyss (Revelation 20). That makes him the beast who rises from the bottomless pit. (Revelation 11 and 17), to drag Gog of Magog (Ezekiel 38, Revelation 11, 16 and 20), to their final judgment. And he is destined to the lake of fire when all is said and done (Revelation 20).

Let us cast off the concerns we carry about our enemy and walk in the power of our risen king, whose first coming defeated the former rulers and set a new kingdom on the move. Let's participate by fulfilling the mandate to go into all the world and make disciples. If you can't go, send. Let's pray for the peace of Israel and fund everything we can to tell them about their king and the kingdom that awaits them. Let's live holy and righteous lives as we hasten the coming of the king. Our mission has been clearly stated, along with the authority by which it is given.

Matthew 28:18-20

"All authority in heaven and on earth has been given to me. [19] Go therefore and make disciples of all nations, baptizing them in the name of the Father and of the Son and of the Holy Spirit, [20] teaching them to observe all that I have commanded you. And behold, I am with you always, to the end of the age."

The four beasts of Daniel 7, that represent four separate kingdoms, are clearly the single Beast of Revelation 13. Their similarities in origin, appearance, and function cannot be ignored. They come from the sea. They appear with seven heads and 10 horns, with the likeness of a lion, bear, and leopard. They make war against the holy ones. These beasts are representative of kingdoms, not earthly kings. They are the spiritual beings that ruled over those kingdoms. See Daniel 10 and its reference to the Princes of Persia and Greece. The following chart demonstrates this.

The Beasts are the Beast, and the Beast is Gog

Daniel 7:1-9 LXX	Revelation 13:1-8
[2] "Upon my bed I saw in a vision while sleeping at night, **and behold, four winds of heaven blew against the great sea.** [3] **And, indeed, four wild beasts arose out of the sea**, each one differing from the other.	[1] And I saw a beast rising out of the sea...

The Beasts are the Beast, and the Beast is Gog

[7] And after these things, as I continued to gaze into the vision during the night, a fourth wild beast...**And it had ten horns.**	[1] And I saw a beast rising out of the sea, **with ten horns** and seven heads, with ten diadems on its horns...
[6] And then after this, as I continued watching, another wild beast, it was just like a leopard, and it had four wings that were stretched out above it, **and the beast had four heads.**[20]	[1] And I saw a beast rising out of the sea, with ten horns **and seven heads**, with ten diadems on its horns...
[4] The first one was **like a lioness** but it had feathers just like an eagle... [5] And indeed, behold, after it another wild beast having the **likeness of a bear**... [6] And then after this, as I continued watching, another wild beast, it was just **like a leopard**...	[2] And the beast that I saw was like a **leopard**; its feet were like a **bear's**, and its mouth was like a **lion's** mouth.

---

[20] 4 beasts, 3 of which have a single while one has four. 7 heads total.

The Beasts are the Beast, and the Beast is Gog

11 At that time I continued to consider the sound of the arrogant assertions that the horn was uttering, and, as **I was looking, the beast was viciously killed** and its body destroyed...	**3** One of its heads seemed to have **a mortal wound**, but its mortal wound was healed...
11 At that time I continued to consider **the sound of the arrogant assertions** that the horn was uttering...	**5** And the beast was given **a mouth uttering haughty and blasphemous words**...
8 ... and it began **to make war against the holy ones.** [21]	**7** Also, it was allowed **to make war on the saints** and to conquer them.[22]

---

[21] ἅγιος (*hagios*) – Holy ones
[22] ἅγιος (*hagios*) – Saints

Now What

Now that you have six rules to help you understand the Revelation, what are you going to do with them?

My hope is that you will begin a fresh read of the Revelation and apply all that you've learned. Make yourself slow down and look for the hundreds of allusions to the Old Testament. When you find them, spend some time there. Learn the Old Testament concepts John applies when he is explaining what he sees. For example, we talked a lot about the four disastrous acts of judgment. They come from Leviticus 26 and are applied in Ezekiel 14. Take some time and explore those chapters and become familiar with them. Chase down similar chapters like Deuteronomy 28 and 29. See how they apply to the history of Israel both before Christ in the Assyrian and Babylonian exiles and then after Christ with the destruction of Jerusalem in 70 AD. Look for things like the horsemen in Zechariah and how they compare to the horsemen of Revelation 6.

Don't forget Daniel 7. It is vitally important to understanding what Jesus accomplished on the cross, and it informs John as he writes the Revelation. We didn't talk about it here, but read Isaiah 24-27 and see what connections you can find. Look at how Isaiah deals with the serpent and then trace down other passages that talk about Leviathan, Rehab, and the dragon. Spend some time in Job 40 and 41 and consider the two beasts God describes there. How, if at all, do they align with the Revelation. The idea is for you to understand how the Old Testament plays a part in understanding John and the other New Testament authors. Remember, some of the rules are universal to the New Testament.

While you're looking around, notice how the Old Testament speaks about the unseen realm. The Elohim, the sons of God, the Cherubim, and so on. Notice how it talks about Leviathan and how it relates to nations like Egypt. There is an unnoticed world happening in the Old Testament. It is veiled by our modern minds. I hope this book will reveal it and bring it into the light. I believe it will help your Bible come to life.

Remember what you've learned about the timing of the Revelation. It's not all in the future. Some of it has happened. Some of it is happening. Some of it is yet to happen. Don't let the news cycle dictate what you believe the Bible is saying. Blood moons and eclipses are not reasons for alarm. These heavenly signs were part of the beginning of the church in Acts 2 when Peter said, *"This is that spoken by the prophet Joel."* Realize that it is more about the host of heaven than anything else. God is dealing with the fallen elohim. What you thought was going to happen is happening and has been happening, and we are meant to be active in it, imaging God and sharing the Gospel and saving some while the world is marked by the beast.

While you're reading the Revelation, I hope you notice the intermissions. I want you to see how the chapters stack on top of each other rather than follow in a linear timeline. See how John revisits key events like the battles I discussed. There are more things repeated through the four acts. Look for the groups of worshippers that appear in the different acts. Notice the different openings of the heavenly temple. It is such a tight story when it is read together using the idea of recapitulation. It is so different from the story I thought it told before. It was disjointed and schizophrenic almost, but now it makes sense, and it matches so well with other parts of the Bible.

Look for the symbolism as you read, but be sure to let the Old Testament inform you about it. When you see lampstands in the Revelation, look for lampstands in the Old Testament. When you see dragons in the Revelation, look for dragons in the Old Testament. When John talks about horsemen, find horsemen in the Old Testament. Some of John's symbols are fully explained by the Old Testament prophets. The minor prophets are a good place to start when you begin to familiarize yourself with the Old Testament.

Lastly, and most importantly, and I've hinted at it above, realize that the Revelation is relevant and practical. Instead of waiting for some form of government to force you to take a mark or prevent you from buying necessities because you refuse, stop taking part in the evil of our current market. Image God, not the beast which is this current world system fueled by the fallen elohim and their demonic hordes. Be like the first-century Christians who voluntarily removed themselves from ungodly markets and feasts. Stop waiting around to take the stand you think you will take when the so-called antichrist appears and take it now. Realize that the tribulation is going on around you right now. Jesus is raging war on his spiritual enemies now, and we can help. Prayer, fasting, generosity, and sharing the gospel, are just some of the ways we can participate in this end times war.

Peter had to address the idea that Jesus had already returned. He assured his readers that he had not. Two thousand years later, the question has changed a bit. Now, people feel like he will never return. The question might be different, but Peter's answer works nonetheless.

> 2 Peter 3:8-13
>
> [8] But do not overlook this one fact, beloved, that with the Lord one day is as a thousand years, and a thousand years as one day. [9] The Lord is not slow to fulfill his promise as some count slowness, but is

patient toward you, not wishing that any should perish, but that all should reach repentance. [10] But the day of the Lord will come like a thief, and then the heavens will pass away with a roar, and the heavenly bodies will be burned up and dissolved, and the earth and the works that are done on it will be exposed.

[11] Since all these things are thus to be dissolved, what sort of people ought you to be in lives of holiness and godliness, [12] waiting for and hastening the coming of the day of God, because of which the heavens will be set on fire and dissolved, and the heavenly bodies will melt as they burn! [13] But according to his promise we are waiting for new heavens and a new earth in which righteousness dwells.

Hasten the coming of the day of God by living lives of holiness and godliness.

God bless you in your studies.

Made in United States
Orlando, FL
13 July 2025